DISCARD

THE *Cry* OF
MORDECAI

BOOKS BY ROBERT STEARNS

Prepare the Way or Get Out of the Way

The Cry of Mordecai

AVAILABLE FROM DESTINY IMAGE PUBLISHERS

THE *Cry* OF MORDECAI

Awakening an Esther Generation in a Haman Age

ROBERT STEARNS

DESTINY IMAGE® PUBLISHERS, INC.
P.O. Box 310, Shippensburg, PA 17257-0310

"Speaking to the Purposes of God for this Generation and for the Generations to Come."

This book and all other Destiny Image, Revival Press, Mercy Place, Fresh Bread, Destiny Image Fiction, and Treasure House books are available at Christian bookstores and distributors worldwide.

For a U.S. bookstore nearest you, call 1-800-722-6774.
For more information on foreign distributors, call 717-532-3040.
Reach us on the Internet at www.destinyimage.com.

ISBN: 0-7684-2754-1
ISBN: 978-0-7684-2754-7
For Worldwide Distribution, Printed in the U.S.A.
2 3 4 5 6 7 8 9 10 / 13 12 11 10 09

DEDICATION

For Ana.
Sweetheart, you are every bit as wise
and beautiful as the heroine of this book,
and I am blessed among men
to have you at my side.

ACKNOWLEDGMENTS

Writing is a great joy for me. I thoroughly enjoy pondering the shades of meaning that words display, and wrestling with inspiration, keyboard, thesaurus, and coffee to try to really say something worthy of your time. If you judge this book deserving of that accolade, please take into account the thanks I owe to the following:

First to my dear grandmother, "Miss Ronnie"—the light of my life. This book (and I) would not be here if not for your faithful prayers. "Thank you" is not enough.

Steve Jenks and Paul and Sue Ten Eyck partner with Ana and me in our leadership of the Eagles' Wings Community, and are heroes who live out their extraordinary diligence in God's work and their faithfulness to stand with me in this vision. I am honored to be in covenant with them.

The whole Eagles' Wings team, who will forgive me for not naming each of them, are a fundamental source of inspiration and joy to me on a daily basis. I know you will say I'm biased, but they really are the best people on earth.

Specifically, Sarah Wolf and Aaron Derstine are owed much of the credit for this book for their research, writing assistance, and editing skills. I deeply appreciate the integrity of their lives, and their dedication to God's Kingdom.

Pastor Chuck Smith of Clarence Center United Methodist Church provided a quiet, bathed-in-prayer place for us to work, for which we are grateful.

I want to thank my dear friends, Gilad Erdan and Ehud Danoch, who are, I believe, Mordecais in the house of Israel at this moment in time. May Israel bravely hear their clear words of leadership and become the Esther she is called to be.

Destiny Image, headed by the tribe of Nori, has been a joy to work with. I appreciate their integrity and dedication to Kingdom work.

ENDORSEMENTS

There is a tremendous need for today's believer to awaken to the world-changing potential and powerful calling that God has placed upon this generation. In *The Cry of Mordecai*, Robert Stearns has issued a stirring call for those who will rise up with great courage and conviction as Esthers in today's world. I highly recommend this timely and motivational book!

Dr. Myles Munroe
President, Bahamas Faith Ministries
International Nassau, Bahamas

Think of it: a vibrant, secure Church awakening the nation to God's Kingdom. As I have traveled extensively throughout the United States speaking to Christian leaders and political pundits, I am convinced that we must understand our true destiny. And this starts with the individuals who are willing to not just dream the American dream but also the Kingdom dream. Robert Stearns has succinctly penned a book on how to become a nation-changer. *The Cry of Mordecai* has captured the essence of the heart of God for every Christian. In allegorical fashion, Robert has buried our excuses and shown us how to resurrect our purpose on earth. Make the pages of this book your prayer and you will do great things!

Bishop Harry R. Jackson Jr.
Senior Pastor of Hope Christian Church
Founder and President, High Impact
Leadership Coalition

Robert Stearns is an extremely gifted leader in the Body of Christ who embodies the message of this book. Like few others on the globe, he has interfaced with leaders in both the Jewish and Christian communities. He is uniquely qualified to write and teach this message regarding Mordecai. It is a timely book in today's global climate.

Dr. Mac Pier
President, NYC Leadership Center
Founder, Concerts of Prayer Greater New York

Unfortunately we all do it—believe that God can use others and doubt that God can use us. In *The Cry of Mordecai* Robert Stearns convincingly and conclusively shows us through Scripture that if God could use Esther, He can use us. This book is a must-read for all who want to step into God's destiny for their lives.

Robert Morris, Senior Pastor
Gateway Church, Southlake, Texas

With clarity and a compelling passion, my friend Robert Stearns has echoed the ancient voice of Mordecai in our present age—a voice that calls the Church not to find its security and comfort in the trappings of our culture. He has communicated this message to our local church, and we received the heart of the message as a wake-up call to fix our attention on Jesus Christ. My prayer is that you will find the awakening, courage, and empowering of Esther to be a reality in your own pursuit of our Great God.

Dr. Jerry Gillis, Lead Pastor
The Chapel at CrossPoint

Esther has been one of my favorite Bible stories since I was a boy. There are so many principles exposed in the story that are relevant for all of us at any stage of life. My friend Robert Stearns offers incredible insights in and subsequent application from the Book of Esther in a way that few could do. I joyfully recommend Robert and this very helpful book to you.

Dr. Paul Cedar, Chairman
Mission America Coalition

Once again God is speaking to His Church through the clear prophetic voice of His chosen servant, Robert Stearns. *The Cry of Mordecai* reads like a modern-day road map for the Church to arise and fulfill Her commission. *The Cry of Mordecai* is a must-read for the Body of Christ if we are to successfully navigate the stormy waters of the 21st century.

Bishop Jim Bolin, Senior Pastor
Trinity Chapel Church of God

Reverend Robert Stearns has written a fascinating commentary on the Scroll of Esther. Yes, Rev. Stearns is a leading voice in the Christian Evangelical movement, but he has also demonstrated the universal quality of this biblical work as well as its enormous relevance for the political situation of Israel today. And although he does extract lessons for the Christian community, he in no way Christianizes the characters of the book who remain Jews throughout.

Rabbi Shlomo Riskin
Founder, Ohr Torah Stone Institutions
and Rabbi of Efrat, Israel

CONTENTS

SPECIAL NOTE FROM THE AUTHOR

Some of the material in this book addresses geo-political realities of our day, and specifically, the issue of radical Islam. As such, I offer the following caveat:

To begin with, there are millions of peaceful Muslims worldwide. They are not interested in jihad or violence of any kind. Oftentimes they are the subject of brutal and murderous attacks at the hand of radical Islam. Some of them are even working to reform Islam and bring it into an understanding commensurate with the modern world. While, as a Christian, I of course pray for them to fully know the love and salvation of Jesus, I nevertheless appreciate their efforts and partnership in standing against the violence of Islamic jihad.

Regarding the millions of non-peaceful Muslims who are part of the radical, murderous Islamic agenda, as a Christian, my command from Jesus is that I love even my enemies. I exhort my fellow believers to join me in loving, praying for, and working toward the salvation of those who are, even now, enemies of the cross of Christ.

> *For we do not wrestle against flesh and blood, but against principalities, against powers, against the rulers of the darkness of this age, against spiritual hosts of wickedness in the heavenly places* (Ephesians 6:12).

THEY CAME FIRST FOR THE COMMUNISTS,
AND I DIDN'T SPEAK UP BECAUSE I WASN'T A COMMUNIST.
THEN THEY CAME FOR THE JEWS,
AND I DIDN'T SPEAK UP BECAUSE I WASN'T A JEW.
THEN THEY CAME FOR THE TRADE UNIONISTS,
AND I DIDN'T SPEAK UP BECAUSE I WASN'T A TRADE UNIONIST.
THEN THEY CAME FOR THE CATHOLICS,
AND I DIDN'T SPEAK UP BECAUSE I WAS A PROTESTANT.
THEN THEY CAME FOR ME,
AND BY THAT TIME NO ONE WAS LEFT TO SPEAK UP.

*—This poem is attributed to Martin Niemoeller,
an influential Lutheran pastor from
World War II Germany who was initially
complicit with Hitler's political agenda
and pledged him the support of the
Protestant churches he represented.
When Niemoeller finally recognized Hitler's true
intentions and realized he was not going to honor
any of the allegiances he had made to the Church,
he withdrew his support from the Nazi party.
He was subsequently arrested and spent the
remainder of the war in a Nazi prison
and eventually the Dachau concentration
camp as one of Hitler's personal prisoners.*

FOREWORD

In working among millions of teenagers in the Church for more than 20 years, one thing I have learned is that it takes a generation of people radically committed to God to change the world.

Sustained passion, godly zeal, and the power to transform society come from seeking God together as a vibrant community of faith, and through working as teammates in the midst of a world of darkness that is desperately in need of the light of the Kingdom of God.

Music, movies, multimedia productions, massive light shows, and stadium events all have their place, but when the hype fades away, a generation must remain to carry the torch and actually do what it takes to change the world.

What does it take to make this happen?

I believe it starts with one life that just won't give up—that one person, an Esther, a Daniel, a passionate believer who loves God too much to throw in the towel when things get tough. One person must stand up and make the decision to do what it takes.

Then, because of that one person who responds to the call and to the need, faith can come upon an entire generation through the courage of that one person who stepped out and took a risk.

You see, it is not enough for us to obey God on our own—we need to become a contagious force for change and bring others with us in our quest to win back this world for God. Radical people will do radical things—especially those who have the burning zeal of God within them like the prophets, judges, and kings and queens throughout Bible history. Radical people aren't afraid to do what needs to be done, even if it hasn't been done before. And they know that, in order to accomplish the task in front of them, they will need the help of others working toward a common goal.

Esther stepped through the open door that God placed before her, and has become one of history's great examples of a risk-taking, God-representing, truth-declaring revolutionary who shaped history. In today's world, we need a company of Esthers to realize they have been called to lead, to provide a model of courage for other believers, and to bring the kind of reformation that can save our society from moral demise.

This book is about changing the world. If ever there was a time that we needed an Esther Generation, it's now. If you're reading this and you desire to make a difference with the life you've been given, allow the zeal that you have inside you to turn into the power necessary to, through God's Spirit, change a nation and to transform a generation.

The world is looking for those who will raise a higher standard of godliness and moral courage, and who will lead with determination and conviction. Millions of people are living their lives without a real purpose, and as you read this, if you have a personal relationship with God, you have living inside you today that purpose that the rest of the world needs. You hold the answer for a generation that is dying without the knowledge of God, and the answer for a world that is perishing without a true experience of who He really is.

Can a nation be changed in a day? Can the world be changed for good? Yes—but it will take a generation of us committed to radical obedience and courageous action in the circumstances in which we find ourselves. Are you ready to do something? Then you, like Esther, are in the right place at the right time.

I invite you to join me as we hear God speak to us out of the pages of an old story—a story that you have probably heard many times before, but which our brother Robert Stearns relays with unique and revolutionary insight. It's the story of an orphan, a king, a people who were on the brink of elimination. Robert draws an important parallel between Esther and the lives of people like you and me today, which I believe holds more significance than we now realize.

Once again, it's time to change the world. *Are you ready?*

Let's do it together and believe for the hearts of the nations of the earth to be turned to worship our great God!

Consumed by the Call,

Ron Luce
Founder and President
Teen Mania Ministries

CHAPTER 1

~

ONE LIFE MAKES ALL THE DIFFERENCE

An unused life is an early death.
—Johann Wolfgang von Goethe

How wonderful it is that nobody need wait
a single moment before starting
to improve the world.[1]
—Anne Frank

"The news is reporting that Benazir Bhutto has been assassinated."

I hung up my cell phone and immediately headed toward a television. As I did, my mind flashed to the recent memory of sitting at lunch with Mrs. Bhutto, the former Prime Minister of Pakistan, at the Presidential Palace in Kiev, Ukraine. We were both speakers at the Inaugural Summit on Peace and Tolerance. I had been privileged to share two private meals with her, and also had several other opportunities for conversation during that three-day conference, which had taken place just eight months earlier.

I had been watching now for many weeks, along with the rest of the world, as she had triumphantly returned to Pakistan and was standing up against the government, calling for fair and democratic elections. Now, watching the news coverage of her death on the screen in front of me felt...it felt surreal. Certainly I did not know her as a close friend; and yet, having spent time with her as she shared her story with me, the tragedy being played out on the television in front of my eyes seemed unbelievable. The juxtaposition of remembering a personal lunch with someone who was sharing about her children and personal aspirations over coffee, and seeing now a world leader assassinated, was mind-numbing.

She told me that her native Pakistan had been filled with turmoil and unrest "forever, it seemed." Her father, brother, and uncle had all been killed. When we were together in May 2007, she was still living in political exile, dividing her time between England (where her son, Bilawal, was studying at Christ Church Oxford), and Dubai, United Arab Emirates, from where she was attempting to stage her political return to Pakistan. She had spoken glowingly and with obvious pride about her son, whose image I now saw on the screen, mourning beside his mother's lifeless body.

She was a strong woman, completely dedicated to her cause. Believing that the fate of her people rested in the decisions she did or did not make, she chose to turn her back on the comfortable life in the West—where she could have given speeches and written books about her experience as the first and only woman to be elected Prime Minister of an Islamic nation—and return to her homeland to fulfill what she believed was her destiny. In so doing, she knew that her death was very possible, and perhaps likely.

This was a woman, a wife, a mother, a leader who chose to fight the forces of radicalism and extremism within Islam, who chose to hear another call and take a difficult path.

~

It is not hard to draw comparisons between the late Benazir Bhutto and the biblical Esther, Queen of Persia. Both gifted, intelligent, beautiful young women who found themselves in high-level positions of national influence at a time when much was at stake. Like Benazir, Esther was a woman who took a stand for her people. Her brave actions ultimately saved the Israelite nation from extinction. These two women had other options in life, but they chose to live for the greater good.

Over the past several years of my life, I have been absolutely captivated by the story of Esther, who was an everyday, ordinary girl, with nothing (other than her beauty) remarkable about her. She possessed no qualities that would set her apart for greatness or political involvement or national leadership. She was an average person who found herself in an historic, world-changing moment. She discovered, through the persistent voice of her Uncle[2] Mordecai, that the events of her life, which had brought her to the palace at that particular point in history, were not arbitrary. She had been positioned by an unseen hand for a yet unknown purpose.

~

Men and women throughout history and today have chosen to make a difference in their world—both for good and for evil. Have you ever thought about how the monumental events of history are inextricably linked with the names, faces, and life stories of commonplace, flesh-and-blood people? No one can tell their children the story of the American Revolution without mentioning the name of Paul Revere. It's impossible to remember the events of 9/11 without envisioning the passport photos of the 19 hijackers who flew the planes into the Twin Towers that Tuesday morning in New York City.

One individual life matters. One individual's choice makes a difference. My life, your life, our lives, and the choices we make every day about how we use the gift of life we have been given, make so much more of an impact than we realize. For better or worse, history really does change because regular, everyday people—mothers, fathers, workers, teachers, grandparents—make decisions to use the resources they have been given to effect change in the world around them. The doors of history hinge on the extraordinary decisions of ordinary people.

THE DOORS OF HISTORY HINGE ~ ON THE EXTRAORDINARY DECI- ~ SIONS OF ORDINARY PEOPLE.

OPENING THE DOOR

It is not a difficult task to prove how history changes, for better or worse, because ordinary people make principled decisions.

How much longer would slavery have been tolerated if William Wilberforce hadn't won his 20-year-long battle to end the British slave trade? The 2007 film, *Amazing Grace*, was a tribute to his Christian faith that prompted him to become passionate about social reform. He and others campaigned for an end to the trade in which British ships were carrying innocent people from Africa, in terrible conditions, to the West Indies as goods to be bought and sold. Wilberforce lobbied with dogged determination for 18 years, and despite the constant censure of his peers in Parliament, he insistently pushed for anti-slavery motions until success was won.[3]

We all think of Dr. Martin Luther King Jr. as the towering prophetic leader of the civil rights movement. A powerful, well-educated orator, he had the charisma to lead perhaps the most massive social justice movement in our nation's history. But don't forget that it is Rosa Parks who is nationally recognized as the "mother of the modern-day civil rights movement" in the United States. Born the daughter of a carpenter and a teacher, Rosa grew up to also become a teacher and married Raymond Parks, a barber. Together they worked behind the scenes through organizations to improve the conditions of their people. Her refusal to surrender her seat to a white male passenger on a Montgomery,

Alabama, bus in 1955 triggered a wave of protests that reverberated throughout the country. The simple, courageous act of a commonplace schoolteacher changed America, its view of African Americans, and redirected the course of world events.[4]

After seeing the conditions outside her classroom window, Mother Teresa left the convent school where she had been teaching to devote herself to working among the poor in the slums of Calcutta. She depended on "Divine Providence" and started an open-air school for disadvantaged children. From humble beginnings, Agnes Gonxha Bojaxhiu (Mother Teresa's given name) dedicated her every thought, desire, and breath to helping the poor. She eventually established the Society of Missionaries that has spread worldwide, including former Soviet Union and Eastern European countries, providing assistance to needy families in Asia, Africa, and Latin America. The religious order left in place by this one faithful woman now offers relief work in the wake of natural catastrophes, such as floods, epidemics, and famine. The order has houses in North America, Europe, and Australia, where they care for shut-ins, alcoholics, homeless, and AIDS sufferers.[5]

The power to make choices that impact the direction of history applies not only to lives committed to righteous causes, but also to those advancing purposes of wickedness. Humankind's natural tendency, when not tempered by the transforming power of absolute truth, is to lust for power and self-gratification. Many in history (and many today) succumb to the evil inclinations within their souls and are led by these tendencies to make a difference in their worlds as well.

In the late 1970s, Pol Pot and his Khmer Rouge party, a prime example of the staggering evil that human nature can generate, killed more than a million Cambodians "to create an idealized agrarian communist society." Along the way, he crushed social institutions such as banking and religion to reach his goal.[6]

In Africa, genocide and tribal wars have left millions dead over the past few decades at the hands of a few corrupt leaders. In 1994, Rwandan Prime Minister, Jean Kambanda—later sentenced to life in prison for his crimes—sanctioned the genocidal slaughter of more than 500,000 minority men, women, and children during a three-month period alone.[7] This tragic occurrence of bloodshed is paralleled by Idi Amin's rule in Uganda in the 1970s, which resulted in the appalling number of at least 100,000 murdered Ugandans—again, in large part, due to the actions of one determined individual.[8]

In 1973, "Jane Roe" (a woman who has since become a vocal, passionate leader in the pro-life movement) challenged abortion regulations and won the court decision. Since then more than 48 million unborn children have ceased to exist in this world. In 2005 alone, there were 1.2 million abortions in the United States.[9] One court decision (instigated by one human being) changed the fate and face of generations who have never had the chance to cure cancer, create art and literature, discover energy-conserving innovations, and advance the population of a freedom-loving nation.

And tragically, horrendously, with echoes of the story of Esther, we come to the "Haman" from one generation past: Adolf Hitler. In 1933, the population of Jews in Europe was more than 9 million. By 1945, two out of every three Jews had been killed because of the pathological hatred of an unimpeded politician.[10] One individual attempted to systematically eradicate an entire ethnic group, and for an entire decade, rational human beings carried out his orders.

HAMAN'S LEGACY OF DESTRUCTION

In the Persian land of Hitler's predecessor, Haman, 25 centuries ago, all seemed well for the Jewish people. Though they were living in exile, they were relatively safe and assimilated into what appeared to be a reasonably comfortable living situation for them. Though they were still considered foreigners,

some of them, like Mordecai, had procured positions of prominence in the land. Nevertheless, underneath this thin veil of
tenuous peace, an evil plot was stirring in the heart of one
man who had become the top official under the authority of
the king of Persia.

Haman is one who set himself on a course to attain the
destruction of the Jewish people. As recorded in the Book of
Esther, Haman approached the king and said of the Jews,
"There is a certain people...let a decree be written that they
be destroyed..." (Esther 3:8-9). He wanted to annihilate this
people "whose customs are different from those of all other
people" (Esther 3:8 NIV). This evil design within him grew,
gained strength (and eventually governmental acceptance),
and seemed insurmountable—until the unlikely intervention of a young, inexperienced queen named Esther and her
caretaker uncle stopped it dead in its tracks.

In the first few decades of the 1900s, Jews in Germany, not
unlike the Jews in Susa, enjoyed unprecedented security and
prosperity as full-fledged members of German society. Highly
assimilated into the life of their nation, they enjoyed great
success in many areas of endeavor—from the political to the
artistic—during what was termed the "Golden Age" of European
Jewry. For example, Hugo Preuss, a Jew greatly skilled in law
and politics, was the primary author of the Weimar Republic's
constitution.[11] Jews held high positions in the Weimar
government and also made great cultural contributions, such as
the playwright Bertolt Brecht who was at the height of his
prolific career in 1920s Germany when his immensely popular
Threepenny Opera premiered in Berlin. The Jews were so
assimilated into their German nation that they represented a
sizable portion (100,000) of the German armed forces in World
War I, in which an estimated 12,000 Jews lost their lives fighting
for their country.[12]

In the years following World War I, as the nation of Germany
moved into a rebuilding phase, life seemed good and comfortable and safe for German Jews. But again, under what seemed to

be ideal circumstances, an evil plot was stirring in the heart of a man—Hitler. Slowly, insidiously, unbelievably, the virus of hatred in his soul became infectious and spread throughout civilized, cultured Germany.

Cartoons ridiculing and mocking the Jewish people became the norm, as Hitler's propaganda machine taught that Jews were an inferior race—the descendants of monkeys and apes. An evil alliance between various sectors of society began to form as Hitler constructed his plan for the complete eradication of European Jewry.

Within Germany, a few courageous voices, like that of Dietrich Bonhoeffer, and the White Rose Society, were raised in alarm, warning the Church and society as a whole of the consequences if Hitler were not confronted—if good people did nothing. But these voices were few and far between. On the political scene, a tug of war ensued in Great Britain between Neville Chamberlain, who advocated appeasement and restraint, and Winston Churchill, who was viewed as a warmonger because he continued to lift his voice and sound an alarm against Hitler's genocidal aggression. Hitler was eventually defeated, but at a cost so great it staggers the mind. Six million Jews were killed in refined, educated Germany, and so recently that there are still, at this very hour, those alive who lived through these horrific events.

~ SIX MILLION JEWS WERE KILLED IN REFINED, EDUCATED GERMANY. ~

Today, only one generation later, radical forces within Islam are calling for nothing less than the destruction of Israel, the United States, and Western civilization as we know it. The president of Iran has made multiple abhorrent and alarming threats in recent years such as: "The skirmishes in the occupied land [Israel] are part of a war of destiny…. As the Imam said, Israel must be wiped off the map."[13] Globally, a well-funded radicalism is

growing within Islamic cultures, spurring countless young people to consider strapping bombs to their chests and blowing
themselves up as homicide bombers.

Just under the veneer of the prosperous American/Western
European culture, a loud, escalating voice is threatening once
again. This time, however, it is not only the Jews, but also the
followers of Christ who are the targets. This radical religious
call for death and destruction comes at the same time when an
increasing secularism and materialism is numbing the soul of
Americans, causing us to be unaware of the impending, swiftly
approaching danger.

Just as Winston Churchill took a stand against Hitler, Esther stood against Haman with conviction and courage.
Churchill stood virtually alone against fascism and renewed
the world's faith in the superiority of democracy. Esther stood
alone against oppression and renewed her people's faith in the
superiority of her God. I am left asking the question, "In another sixty years, what will students be reading in their textbooks about the totalitarian threat we are facing today? Will
there be an Esther, a Churchill who speaks out in our day?"

WILL THERE BE AN ESTHER, A CHURCHILL WHO SPEAKS OUT IN OUR DAY?

KAIROS MOMENTS

The Bible, cover to cover, is the story of ordinary people
encountering and becoming part of the plan of an extraordinary
God. It is the story of everyday people living everyday lives, who
suddenly realize that they are part of something bigger,
something urgent, something that requires them to act, and to
act courageously. Being in the right place at the right time and

making the right decision causes a *kairos* moment—a moment in which time and destiny intersect.

There are two Greek words for time: *chronos* (from which we derive the term "chronological time"), but also the word *kairos*. *Kairos* means "a time when conditions are right for the accomplishment of a crucial action: the opportune and decisive moment."[14]

A countless number of average people throughout time have stood in a moment of decision and seized their "*kairos* moment."

Abraham, for instance, was in the right place at the right time when God said, "To your descendants I will give this land." So Abraham built an altar to the Lord (see Gen. 12:7). Moses' mother stepped into a *kairos* moment when she hid her son for three months and then placed him in a tar and pitch-coated basket, preserving him for his destiny as a leader and deliverer of God's people (see Exod. 2:2-3).

Noah, right in step with the timing of God, began building the ark more than a year before a drop of the flood's rains fell. Following God's direction, the humble carpenter's preparations were right on time—*kairos time*—as the doors of the ark slammed shut and the heavens burst open (see Gen. 6:13–7:10). Noah's obedience saved his family, who were the only remnant people walking in obedience to God in the earth.

Little did Joseph's brothers know that selling him to a passing caravan was part of a divine orchestration of events, preparing their younger brother to be positioned to have authority over all the food supply in Egypt. Joseph, just one of many sons from an ordinary family, grew to be a man who, at an opportune time, saved his entire people from being wiped out by famine (see Gen. 37:25-28; Gen. 42–46).

Joshua was no one special when Moses chose him to be his assistant. But for a predestined purpose and a specified time, God was setting Joshua apart to fulfill the promises of old and to lead His people into the covenant land. After Moses died and the torch was passed to Joshua, the Lord spoke to him at the moment of fulfillment, "Be strong and of good courage, for to this people you shall divide as an inheritance the land which I swore to their fathers to give them" (Josh. 1:6).

Gideon and his small group of 300 men faced thousands of Midianite enemy soldiers coming against the Israelite nation. One night, in obedience to God, they lit torches, blew trumpets, and shouted, then watched as the enemy panicked, and the Lord caused the opposing troops to begin fighting and killing each other (see Judg. 7:19-23), all because Gideon trusted in the Lord's ways and His timing.

The lonely shepherd boy sitting by himself in the fields with only his sheep to keep him company was dismissed by his father for a role that would change the course of history. Yet God was at work in David's life, preparing him and shaping him for his future as the most venerated king of all time. Not only would David become king of Israel, but in the fullness of time David's kingly line was to bring forth the Messiah, establishing David's throne forever and ever (see 1 Sam. 16:7-13; 17:33-50; Ps. 89:3-4).

God uses people throughout generations to fulfill His purpose for them—in His perfect timing. At these pivotal moments, it is as if the heavens and earth both hold their breath in awe at the workings of God through humble humanity, bringing about divine destiny.

Clearly, the Bible relays real stories of real people who had to make real and tough decisions in order to cooperate with Heaven and push back darkness by advancing the Kingdom of light. We serve the same God today. He is still looking for one: for you, for me, for anyone to come into agreement with His purpose, His values, His plan. Will we make a difference? Will we take a stand?

~ HE IS STILL LOOKING FOR ONE:
FOR YOU, FOR ME, FOR ANYONE
TO COME INTO AGREEMENT
WITH HIS PURPOSE. ~

I am convinced that the principles at work in the story of Esther are timeless, and especially relevant for us today, both individually and corporately. I invite you to join me in taking a fresh look at this ancient story, and listen for the voice of the Spirit speaking to our hearts.

A special word as we take a fresh look at the story of Esther— especially to the men reading this book. Many times the story of Esther is presented with a focus on the romantic, fairy-tale-like quality of the story. In contrast to what you may be expecting, I would like to present a different perspective—one as sure to intrigue as it is to inspire. The focus is not on frills and lace, but on how Esther navigated through the political minefield of court and arranged for the assassination of her enemies. The message of Esther is not gender-specific. God is calling all of us to be world changers.

God, today, is looking for one life to make a difference in a world ever deteriorating into a state of havoc and despair. He is looking for *one* life that He can work through to chart the course for His eternal plan, and through which He can show that He is still on the throne. Esther's (the orphan queen) was one such life. Why not yours?

ENDNOTES

1. http://www.quotegarden.com/helping.html.

2. In Esther 2:7 (NKJV), we are told that Esther was Mordecai's uncle's daughter (his cousin). Because of the apparent age difference between Mordecai

and Esther, we will refer to him as her uncle, as this term more befits the type of relationship they would have had.

3. William Wilberforce (1759-1833); http://www.bbc.co.uk/history/historic_figures/wilberforce_william.shtml; accessed 6/2/08.

4. Rosa Parks (1913-2005); http://www.rosaparks.org/; accessed 6/2/08.

5. Mother Teresa (1910-1997); http://nobelprize.org/nobel_prizes/peace/laureates/1979/teresa-bio.html; accessed 6/2/08.

6. Pol Pot (1928-1998); http://www.time.com/time/daily/polpot/1.html; accessed 6/2/08.

7. James C. McKinley Jr., "Ex-Rwandan Premier Gets Life in Prison on Charges of Genocide in '94 Massacres," NYTimes.com; Sept. 5, 1998, http://query.nytimes.com/gst/fullpage.html?res=9A05EED9163EF936A3575AC0A96E958260; accessed 8/30/08.

8. Uganda background notes, U.S. State Department, http://www.state.gov/r/pa/ei/bgn/2963.htm; accessed 8/30/08.

9. Abortions: http://www.nrlc.org/abortion/facts/abortionstats.html; accessed 6/2/08.

10. Adolf Hitler (1889-1945); http://www.ushmm.org/wlc/article;php?lang=en&ModuleId=10005143; accessed 6/2/08.

11. "Hugo Preuss," Encyclopaedia Britannica Online, http://original.britannica.com/eb/article-9061316/Hugo-Preuss#74896.hook; accessed 8/30/08.

12. Martin Gilbert, *The Jews in the Twentieth Century* (New York: Schocken Books, 2001), 71.

13. "Ahmadinejad quotes," May 16, 2006, jpost.com, http://www.jpost.com/servlet/Satellite?cid=1145961353170&pagename=JPost/JPArticle/ShowFull; accessed 8/30/08.

14. Kairos; http://www.allwords.com/word-kairos.html.

CHAPTER 2

~

THREE STRIKES

In Jewish history there are no coincidences.[1]
—Elie Wiesel

Imagine for a moment that you woke up this morning to find that, overnight, you had become one of the wealthiest, most influential people in the country. You had all the material things you wanted—cars, boats, clothes, houses, all the food you could eat, all the attention you craved—notoriety, fame, recognition, status. In short, you had everything you ever dreamed of. That was Esther the day after being chosen.

You probably remember the basics of her story: The king had grown angry with his wife, Vashti, and she had been deposed. So the king sent out a message throughout his realm that he was looking for a new queen. To put it in modern terms, Ryan Seacrest went to shopping malls across America looking for the next big thing. The quest to find the new Queen of Persia was the "American Idol" of its day and all the eligible young women were rounded up and paraded before Paula, Simon, and Randy.

We're told that Esther was born lovely in appearance, "beautiful of form and face" (Esther 2:7 NASB), so she gained favor before the judges and was taken to the king's palatial estate. In one moment, this little orphan girl who had only ever known despair, doubt, and meager means was transported to a world of extravagance, power, and affluence. In the blink of an unpainted eye, she went from Wal-Mart to Neiman Marcus. Simple, uneducated, unrefined, this young girl who knew nothing of palace protocol, nothing of political influence, nothing of opulence, was brought from obscurity into the highest realm.

Esther had been assigned seven maids who were at her beckoning and charged with helping her become queenly. She bathed in myrrh and frankincense and indulged in all the latest beauty treatments available in her day. She was transported from complete anonymity to total celebrity status. What euphoria she must have experienced in discovering her newfound identity!

But lurking in the shadows of Esther's past were three debilitating setbacks, which still had the power to threaten and haunt her, and which could very easily derail her as she stepped into her unfolding destiny. What I have found, and what I believe you will find in looking at these three core issues, is that they are timeless, still every bit as formidable today as they were when Esther confronted them centuries ago.

THE POWER OF WEAKNESS

Weakness can be an invitation to greatness. We serve a God who declares in His Word, "My grace is sufficient for you, for My strength is made perfect in weakness" (2 Cor. 12:9a). We serve the God of Moses the stutterer, David the adulterer, Joseph the dreamer, Elijah the scared, Gideon the youngest, and Esther the orphan.

A piece of dirt, of sand, finds its way past the hard outer protective shell of an oyster, deep into the folds of the heart of flesh, and this piece of dirt, this irritant, this unwelcome intrusion becomes, in time, the costly pearl within the oyster. The oyster itself is transitory—a temporary blip on the ocean floor—but the result of the pain it endured will be cherished and passed on from generation to generation, often adorning the neck of a bride.

When we encounter Esther, there is nothing about her that leads us to believe she will move into prominence. Esther is the original Cinderella. She is alone, insignificant, and seems to have every disadvantage. She has not been born into the right family; she has not attended the right schools. In fact, there are three very distinctive burdens she carries, which, like sand in an oyster, are serious irritants, making it seem likely that her life will be, at best, unremarkable and, at worst, quite difficult.

~ ESTHER IS THE ORIGINAL CINDERELLA. ~

So many times we read stories of Bible characters and we revel in the victory of their outcomes. But what I love about Scripture is that it paints such a very real, honest picture of our heroes and heroines. Scripture does not whitewash or ignore people's faults, difficulties, or shortcomings. Why?

I believe it is because God is saying to us, *"You can do it, too! I know about your failures; I know about your struggles. None of them have caught Me by surprise. The things that you want no one to know about, and that you try to hide even from yourself, are not obstacles to My love or My destiny for your future. In fact, I have allowed some of those very difficulties and will redeem them to bring about your greater good and blessing."*

39

The three primary setbacks in Esther's life are issues that many of us face in our lives today. Esther was, first of all, *an orphan*. She was also *a woman in a man's world*, and last but certainly not least, she was a *Jew*—"three strikes" in the Persian world of 500 B.C.

These are three strikes, which (like all strikes), had she wallowed in self-pity or stewed in bitterness, would have kept her from ascending into the full realization of her calling. Instead, she allowed these issues to become the very platform on which she would stand in deliverance on behalf of her nation.

STRIKE ONE: ESTHER, THE ORPHAN (FAMILY)

The fact that Esther is an orphan is an often overlooked, glossed-over portion of this amazing narrative. Esther found herself forsaken in this world. Lonely. Without connection or a place to call home. Esther never knew a mother's love. She could not draw from the well of a father's wisdom. She did not know affection, care, camaraderie, or "place." There are many tragedies in life, but surely, one of the greatest is to be alone. Isolated. Without a sense of belonging.

Esther grew up with a great deficit, a great gaping hole in her heart of what it meant to live and grow and be nurtured by a loving, caring family. Esther grew up, like too many of us grow up today, amid much pain, turmoil, and dysfunction. Although Mordecai was a good man, he wasn't her mother or even her father.

Most of us have parents and families, but we may be orphans still. Broken homes and dysfunctional families are the norm in society today. Unfortunately, a stable, blessed home life and family unit is a rarity. When the pain of a broken family causes us to be orphaned in heart, it strikes at the very depths of who we are and what we feel we can become in life. And family pain does not quickly loosen its grip. We never stop wondering, *Why me?* We see others' families, others' relationships, and wish and pray that they were ours.

So many times in Scripture, we see trials such as betrayal, illness, and abandonment in the upbringing of some of God's fiercest heroes. Again, Scripture does not whitewash the stories; and this is a gift to us, because they speak to us in our situations right now. We can identify, across the pages of time, with someone else's private pain.

Have you had a "strike" against you in your family situation? Chances are you have. Most likely there is some situation in your family life—even in the life of families of strong faith—which has caused you pain, disappointment, frustration, or loss. Esther understood this. She lived this. She was alone.

What do we do with our "family pain"? The pain of divorce, abuse, of the prodigal child or grandchild, the loved one who died too soon, the absentee parent, the alcoholic? Nothing strikes so close to home for any of us, as circumstances like these. Even after many years, even after relatives have passed on, we often find ourselves contending for the freedom we know is ours to claim.

Esther's story is powerful to us not because it is a fairy tale, but because it is real. And part of its reality—and most likely in some way, part of your reality—is that she had pain in her heart about her family. Strike one.

But this was not the only challenge she faced in life. Each of us longs for a sense of security and protection. We want to have the feeling that our world is stable and well-grounded. We want to be secure in our finances, our health, our careers, and our homes. A confident sense of peace, safety, and hope for a good future is foundational to our happiness. And yet, what did Esther face? Esther's second major obstacle: she was a woman in a man's world.

STRIKE TWO: ESTHER, THE WOMAN (SECURITY)

My friend Kathy, a very successful senior-level banking executive, was sharing with me recently all she has had to go through to build a significant career in the male-dominated world of executive financial management. She has been told point blank that "the boys [of business] are going to run you out of town." Thankfully, through grace, she has learned to stand her ground and has become known for her resilience, diligence, and excellence.

But if Kathy has had to face challenges as a woman living in the United States in the 21st century, what did Esther face as a woman living in Persia 500 years before the birth of Christ?

Being a woman during that time meant functioning in a severely limited capacity in life. Women were forbidden to own a business, attend school, or get a job. A woman's only real option in life was marriage, which meant having a dowry. As an orphan, Esther had no parents, and hence, no provision for a dowry to secure a marriage. Therefore, her future was uncertain—dependent on her aging uncle.

As we move through life, each of us has an inborn desire to secure a future for ourselves and our children. This is a right and God-given desire. And yet, many times this drive for security becomes relentless and habitual and unthinking. How secure are our lives anyway? How secure were the lives of those with great careers at the top of the World Trade Center on 9/11/2001? Or those who owned homes in the Louisiana bayou when Hurricane Katrina struck? Or any of us as we get into our cars and trust others on the highway as we drive to work, school, or the grocery store?

While it is not wrong to seek a certain level of security in life, it is necessary to remember that, ultimately, security in this world is an illusion. No one is going to get out of here alive! And while we may have a degree of potential influence over the length or quality of our physical lives, why pass from this world never having dared? Never having dreamed? Never having attempted...risked...*jumped*?

~ # SECURITY IN THIS WORLD ~
IS AN ILLUSION.

So many today, even believers, are placing their security in things and people. But ultimately God is our true source, and His Kingdom's economy really is our standard. He calls us not to survival, but to greatness; not to enjoy history from the illusion of secure sidelines, but to place ourselves on the field of battle, in the thick of the fight.

Esther understood this at the end of her journey; but starting out, she was a girl with no financial security, no prospects, and no options. Soon she would be given everything she could have ever hoped for and more—the most prized security this world can offer. And then she would be asked to risk losing it all—everything, even life itself—to answer the cry.

STRIKE THREE: ESTHER, A JEW (IDENTITY)

The third strike Esther faced lay in her heritage. Being a Jew (at a time when, as most times in history, indeed a time like today in too many places), put her in danger and caused her even more adversity. Mordecai cautioned her not to tell anyone that she was a Jew so as to keep her from harm. She was a victim of discrimination in a society that didn't receive or accept her. Don't think that anti-Semitism started with Christianity—the enemy has been out to destroy the Jewish people long before those calling themselves Christians became one of the vehicles of his vendetta.

Esther was a member of a minority population in Persia, formerly the Babylonian Empire that was conquered by armies commanded by Cyrus and Darius. What is now Iran and Afghanistan, was first Assyria, then Babylon, and in Esther's time, Persia. All these Mesopotamian empires had—not always pleasant—interactions with the Jewish people.

How often did Esther feel "different," not like those around her? How often did she feel like an outsider? How often have you felt like an outsider—wishing, hoping, praying that you could fit in and be part of the crowd? Everyone from time to time feels out of place, out of sorts, out of the know.

Esther was living in exile. It would seem very possible, from what we know of her, that she may have been estranged even from her own faith. Her religion might have been a distant memory, now that she was disconnected from her Temple and her people's homeland. Mordecai warned her many times from a young age not to tell anyone she was a Jew. And yet, *he* told her she was a Jew. Why not abandon Judaism altogether? Lose the baggage? Deny the inconvenient truth?

Scripture makes it clear that the danger Haman was about the unleash upon the Jews came, at least in part, because Mordecai clung to the Jewish belief that he should not bow down to anyone other than his God.

> *After these things King Ahasuerus promoted Haman, the son of Hammedatha the Agagite, and advanced him and set his seat above all the princes who were with him. And all the king's servants who were within the king's gate bowed and paid homage to Haman, for so the king had commanded concerning him. But Mordecai would not bow or pay homage. Then the king's servants who were within the king's gate said to Mordecai, "Why do you transgress the king's command?" Now it happened, when they spoke to him daily and he would not listen to them, that they told it to Haman, to see whether Mordecai's words would stand; for Mordecai had told them that he was a Jew. When Haman saw that Mordecai did not bow or pay him homage, Haman was filled with wrath. But he disdained to lay hands on Mordecai alone, for they had told him of the people of Mordecai. Instead, Haman sought to destroy all the Jews who were throughout the whole kingdom of Ahasuerus—the people of Mordecai* (Esther 3:1-6).

So we have this interesting paradox—Mordecai and Esther both clinging to and hiding their Jewish heritage. And so often, isn't this true of us in the Church? Rather than celebrating the greatness of being part of a Kingdom that is "not of this world" (John 18:36), don't we too often try to have the Church "fit in" with the culture, wanting people to know we are "normal," just like they are? Doesn't the Church all too often settle for compromise instead of standing in the place of being "in, but not of" this world (see John 17:11,14)? Like Esther, we become confused about our role. We are part of a community that will not bow down, but we also try to hide that reality under a bushel. After all, the problematic truth could, in the long run, be dangerous for us.

No one feels more acutely the desire to fit in than someone who already, as an orphan and a defenseless dependant, desperately needs to fit in. Family, security, identity. Three core issues that touch each of us at the heart—three determining factors that speak to our very existence. And for Esther, each of these areas was a source of hurt and lack. Yet without these realities, she would not have been uniquely positioned by God to perform the acts of courage that would lead to the salvation of her people.

BRINGING IT HOME

Everyone likes the end of Esther's story when she saves her people from destruction, but many forget her humble beginnings and the enormous challenges she faced along the way. The truth is, most of us have had less-than-stellar beginnings just like hers. Maybe we didn't have the most caring or loving parents, or the opportunity to attend the most prestigious college (or any college at all). Maybe we have been scarred by a world that would rather not have us in it. But *thanks be to God* we serve a Savior who is a Redeemer and Restorer! Our God delights in taking things that are not and making them as they are to be (see Rom. 4:17). He takes our weaknesses and turns them into strengths that will thrust us forward into the adventure of faith He has mapped out for us.

It is all too tempting to fall into the enemy's scheme of seeing the trials we have endured as stumbling blocks from our past rather than stepping stones to our future. We would do well to remember that Esther, while she had no family to surround and comfort her, when the call came to go to the palace, she also had no one to hold her back. She had no pressing responsibilities to slow her down. She could risk her life with focus and determination without worrying how it would affect anyone else.

> IT IS ALL TOO TEMPTING TO FALL INTO THE ENEMY'S SCHEME OF SEEING THE TRIALS WE HAVE ENDURED AS STUMBLING BLOCKS RATHER THAN STEPPING STONES.

While her connection to the Jewish community was the very thing that endangered her life, their identification with her in her three-day fast is what moved the heart of God to respond with His plan for their rescue (see Esther 4:16).

And finally, if her parents had not died before their time, she never would have been sent to live with her Uncle Mordecai, unbetrothed and unwanted by any suitors, free to respond to the royal summons to the king's court.

All the forces conspiring against her, making it appear that she had been dealt a bad hand in life, were actually the means that would propel her into what her life was really all about. When you think of the blows the enemy has brought to bear on your soul, remember this: *if Esther had never been an orphan, she may have never become a queen.* Perhaps then, as well as now, it takes knowing what you're made *of* to know what you're made *for.*

God's infinite wisdom and poetic justice far transcend the wiles of the enemy of our soul. All that now seems hopeless, pointless, and utterly fruitless are merely the temporal conditions that will secure our eternal destinies.

Like Joseph (who virtually holds the world record on suffering unjustly) says to his treacherous brothers when they come to him years after betraying him, "As for you, you meant evil against me, but God meant it for good in order to bring about this present result, to preserve many people alive" (Gen. 50:20 NASB). That, my friends, is seeing your life from a heavenly perspective!

Are you facing three strikes...or more? What has struck at you? Where have you been wounded? Hurt? Treated unfairly? I promise you, on the authority of God's Word, that if you offer up the areas of brokenness and difficulty in your life, our God—the Faithful Father—will take the bleakest moments of your life and make them shine like the noonday sun. Our God is the Redeemer who will turn your mess into your message and your test into your testimony. Praise God that He does not chart our future by our past!

"For I know the thoughts that I think toward you, says the Lord, thoughts of peace and not of evil, to give you a future and a hope" (Jer. 29:11). It doesn't matter what type of trials and traumas you've faced or that you are facing. Ultimately, the very things you have struggled with will be used by God as the tools to prepare you to participate in His Kingdom purposes. That which disqualifies us in the eyes of the world is exactly what God is looking for to choose us for His team. Thankfully, with God, it's three strikes and you're *in*!

~

In the next two chapters, we will look at two widespread deterrents that can prevent us from stepping into the hope-filled future that God has for us. These two obstacles are distraction and denial. Each one, though deadly, can be overcome if we learn to see from God's perspective as Esther did, and receive His Word into our hearts. Join me as we take a journey into Esther's world so that we, too, can walk in the profound victory that she experienced.

ENDNOTE

1. http://www.allgreatquotes.com/jewish_jew_quotes.shtml.

CHAPTER 3

~

THE DANGER OF DISTRACTION

*What good fortune for governments that
the people do not think.*[1]
—Adolf Hitler

In the Western world, we are drowning in distraction.

Television. The Internet. Movies. The mall. Text messaging. IPods. Cell phones. When have we ever been so bombarded with distracting beeps, buzzers, flashes, sounds, messages, pop-ups, and just plain noise? Advertising companies have designed entire campaigns around the premise that if they can just distract you and hold your attention long enough, you will most likely end up buying something from them. Our entire society is actually built upon distraction, which is essentially competition for your attention, e.g., your money. And as we know, "time is money," so to get your money, they actually get your time—your life—your soul.

With all the noise and flashy commercials of modern life, I believe that a deadly combination of both outer and inner distraction is placing us in a stranglehold of ineffectiveness.

In a different age of history, Esther faced a monumental amount of distractions when she was catapulted from her humble life as an orphan into the luxurious life of a queen. As she ascended to her position of influence, she encountered outer distractions of a lifestyle in the palace where "the couches were of gold and silver on a mosaic pavement of alabaster, turquoise, and white and black marble," where "they served drink with golden vessels, each vessel being different from the other, with royal wine in abundance," and where "they should do according to each man's pleasure" (Esther 1:6-8).

On the surface everything was perfect for Esther. She was basking in a miracle story of blessing, which only God Himself could write. As the most important woman in the land, don't you think Esther may have been just a little distracted? Esther now faced the common snare of allowing the blessing of God to distract her from the God of blessing.

~ ESTHER FACED THE SNARE OF AL-
LOWING THE BLESSING OF GOD
TO DISTRACT HER FROM
THE GOD OF BLESSING. ~

INNER DISTRACTIONS

I believe there is more to Esther's situation than meets the eye. Imagine with me for a moment the transition in Esther's inner thought patterns as she made the jump from orphan to queen. Such major adjustment from one world to another could not have happened easily! What went through her mind? What thoughts did she have to fight against that would cause her to doubt her worthiness and capability for her new role?

Think back to the "three strikes" against Esther. How did these insecurities play with her thoughts? Did she still struggle with feeling like an orphan? Now surrounded with people, she was suddenly more alone than ever. And it seemed even more urgent now than before that she hide her Jewish identity. How did this inner fear affect her daily life?

While these inner voices are working overtime to cloud Esther's consciousness, enter now the voice of Mordecai her trusted relative. As we will see even more clearly later in the book, Esther is not able to initially hear his message of warning to her because her distractions erected a shield within her against the truth of her situation. His words cannot fully penetrate her thinking because her heart is not in a position to receive the truth spoken to her. Mordecai's warning can only reach her to the extent that she is able to ward off the voices within that compete against the truth.

Besides the multitude of outer distractions that our contemporary world bombards us with, we all have to deal with the inner distractions, conscious and subconscious, of thought patterns which, unchecked, can become what we call our "personality." Unless we take a long, hard look at how we are thinking, we can be very unaware of how distracted and out of touch with our deepest selves we really are.

For example, I have been blessed to have had numerous experiences meeting and speaking with people of great power and influence. I have met several heads of state, governmental leaders, members of royalty, and people of tremendous earthly power. I remember in my earlier years, when God began opening these doors for me, feeling like I was utterly out of place, and not knowing what to say or how to react in these situations. I would often "freeze up" and miss moments of great opportunity, because I simply was not inwardly prepared.

But I began to realize that the root of this "paralysis" was an inner distraction of fear and insecurity. I began to accept the fact and responsibility that God was putting me in these places and in front of these people for a purpose, and I needed to get over my feelings of inadequacy, and instead prepare to maximize each opportunity the Lord entrusted to me.

In following the calling of God, there are many voices that would seek to distract us from our moments of opportunity. These distractions come in all shapes and sizes, because the enemy of our souls is looking for every way possible to nullify us and to prevent the kind of impact he knows we're capable of making. I can only imagine that Esther's mind, in the midst of her newfound position, was literally *spinning* with the distraction of both the outer opulence and the inner strain that happens when we are called to something that is bigger than we had ever dreamed possible.

Our thoughts are the most basic element of our human experience. Examined and harnessed to purpose, our thoughts become the power source for our life's direction. Unchecked and random, they can become one of the greatest stumbling blocks to walking out our calling. Houses of thought are strongholds either for the blessing of God or the entanglements of the enemy, and many times both of these realities are working simultaneously within us.

~ **HOUSES OF THOUGHT ARE STRONG- HOLDS EITHER FOR THE BLESSING OF GOD OR THE ENTANGLEMENTS OF THE ENEMY.** ~

Our actions are an outflow of our thoughts. Do you want to change your life? Change your actions. Do you want to change your actions? Change your thoughts and speech.

As I travel to minister to the Body of Christ today (in the United States and internationally), I am shocked and even alarmed by how often we who call ourselves believers really don't think according to the mindset of the redeemed. We say that we believe the Bible, but when it comes right down to it, inside our minds we are vastly distracted from what is true and right—from the *basic level* things that the Kingdom of God is really all about.

Scripture exhorts us in Philippians 4:8:

Whatever things are true, whatever things are noble, whatever things are just, whatever things are pure, whatever things are lovely, whatever things are of good report, if there is any virtue and if there is anything praiseworthy—meditate on these things.

To be honest, we are often more concerned about what people think of us than what the Word of God says. We are too focused on maintaining good appearances rather than being inwardly transformed. We are so fearful of natural outcomes that we neglect to operate in the faith that God desires us to walk in. We are often inwardly jealous of others, discontent, and bitter; rather than peaceful, at rest, joyful.

Don't give the adversary room to work in your life! Change how you think. Thoughts are like strongholds that are built up within us, and if we build our inner "house" out of thoughts that do not align with God's Word, we are actually aligning ourselves with darkness and inviting the enemy to bring confusion and weakness into our thought patterns.

"I will never be good enough."

"I can never be fully healed from my past."

"If it wasn't for what he/she did, I wouldn't be facing this hardship right now."

What comes out of our mouths is often the fruit of defense mechanisms that we subconsciously employ as our fleshly nature wages war against the truth of the Kingdom of God. Defense mechanisms mask the pain we feel inwardly, so that we are incapable of acknowledging it, working through it, and moving on. The enemy knows the power of inner distraction, and so he tries to keep us bound up in lie-based thinking that is contrary to the liberating principles of God's Word.

Is it any wonder we don't see the power of God moving more evidently in our lives, when we are not thinking His thoughts but instead are entertaining our own carnal attitudes of jealousies, hurts, and fears, which actually amount to idolatry?

What self-limiting perceptions are you giving authority to in your thought life? Where are you allowing the enemy to play subconscious "tapes" in your mind, over and over again like a broken record? What inner voices are obstructing you from moving forward in your calling?

You really do have a divine purpose. Your life really can and does make a difference. You might not feel it, you might not realize it, but God really wants to make more of you than you have attained so far. He is inviting you to break free from distracting noise, and hear pure, clear sound. The sound of His voice, His Spirit, clarifying your calling, and your next steps.

While the enemy likes to keep us entangled in old cycles, God's plan is to break us out of these and teach us how to think like sons and daughters of God—like royalty.

Our answer is found in the power of the Word of the Lord to dispel lies:

> For the word of God is living and powerful, and sharper than any two-edged sword, piercing even to the division of soul and spirit, and of joints and marrow, and is a discerner of the thoughts and intents of the heart (Hebrews 4:12).

> For though we walk in the flesh, we do not war according to the flesh. For the weapons of our warfare are not carnal but mighty in God for pulling down strongholds, casting down arguments and every high thing that exalts itself against the knowledge of God, bringing every thought into captivity to the obedience of Christ (2 Corinthians 10:3-5).

Like Esther, we must learn to overcome old, limiting patterns of thought so that we can receive the "mind of Christ" (1 Cor. 2:16).

OUTER DISTRACTIONS

Our lives today in the 21st century are filled with an abundance of outward distractions, which seek to keep us from moving forward in God's plan. Many times these things are not evil in and of themselves, but nevertheless end up stealing our focus and robbing us of precious time that could be used to advance us into all He wants to give us.

Outer distractions are symptoms of inner distractions, which have taken root in us individually and as a society. Society's distractions don't originate on their own. Rather, they spring from unresolved issues in the hearts of countless men and women, forming a web of corporate distraction. These outer symptoms (that create a "culture of distraction") have the power to multiply and create more choices and more options that have little or nothing to do with the purpose for which we were created. Like cancer, they multiply rapidly, and form a network of anesthetization.

We live by the inner lie that faster activity and more of it is better. More things, more stuff, now, immediately—in fact, *yesterday* would be good. And indeed, in some ways, things and speed can be a blessing. But they can also enable the condition of distraction, which, regrettably, can be a fatal condition.

DEATH BY DISTRACTION

When you consider what has taken place in the history of the world in only the last one to two hundred years (in comparison with the several *thousands* of years previously), it is utterly astonishing.

Electricity is made available in every home in the West; automobiles are introduced into the fabric of everyday society; the groundbreaking invention of the telephone gives way to the widespread rise of cellular phones; transportation through flight progresses from the Wright brothers' inventions to hundreds of daily commercial flights across the globe; typewriters are replaced by computers and printing presses that release thousands of copies of books per day; new advances in engineering result in space exploration that sends Neil Armstrong to the moon, making what was inconceivable for our grandparents now commonplace. Just think of what they would say if they found out that, for the right fee, they could now purchase their own tickets as space tourists to the outer edges of our galaxy!

What we today take for granted has simply never existed in thousands and thousands of years of human development. Today we can go farther and faster than our forebears would have ever dreamed possible. How is this affecting the human race?

A mere 20 years ago, there was scarcely a soul who knew what the Internet was. Now information is only as far away as your keyboard, of which you may have several in your household. The Internet provides news, weather, dating, shopping, live chat, broadcasts, and a host of other services—essentially an entire technological world complete with anything one could imagine. As of March 2008 there were about 210 million Internet users in the United States and 1.4 billion users worldwide.[2] No longer are people distracted only by what is happening down the street—now they can become instantaneously aware of what's happening in Istanbul or Malaysia.

In the midst of this flurry of never-ending activity, the instability of distraction is on the rise—24 hours a day, 7 days a week. The unsettled soul now has a thousand options to try to fill the inner void that is crying out for meaning. Is it any wonder that a book title such as *The Purpose-Driven Life* would sell millions of copies in this world of escalating, teeming commotion and confusion?

So now we can text people we meet online in China, but we don't know our neighbors. We are more technologically advanced, but far less civil, less humane, less human.

ENTERTAINMENT

Hollywood is a world unto itself that is sustaining and thriving on the condition of distraction in society today. Entertainment has become a multi *billion*-dollar enterprise in our generation; not only a diversion, but a way of life and a steady diet for the diversion-obsessed public. Amazingly, box office revenues in 2007 alone in the U.S. totaled $10.2 billion, nearly twice the entire Gross Domestic Product of the nation of Nicaragua.[3]

Similarly, television, which has defined a generation, has risen to the point where Americans watch an average of 4 hours and 35 minutes of television per day, in households where televisions now outnumber people.[4] How is this affecting us? What is this doing to us? To our children?

Even the world of sports, though admirable for qualities such as teamwork and perseverance, has taken over our minds to the point where multiple ESPN channels deliver people's entertainment cravings at any time of the day or night.

Consider the fact that if someone shouts as a form of worship in a church service, that person is, in most circles, considered abnormal; yet sports fans don't think twice about thousands of people painting themselves myriad colors and spending hundreds of dollars for tickets to games at which they scream at the top of their lungs until they lose their voice. This behavior is considered acceptable in our society, but those who get excited and emotional about God and His Kingdom are viewed with morbid suspicion.

It's increasingly common for families to organize their entire schedules around their kids' soccer tournaments, and if church attendance falls by the wayside, then so be it. The priorities of our hearts are revealed by two things: how we spend our time and our money, and in the case of sports and other forms of entertainment, I fear that, though our mouths profess one thing, it is all too evident where our treasure lies.

> ~ THE PRIORITIES OF OUR HEARTS ARE REVEALED BY TWO THINGS: HOW WE SPEND OUR TIME AND OUR MONEY. ~

"Christian entertainment," now an enormous financial industry just like "worldly entertainment," can be no less a distraction than its secular counterpart. How is shelling big bucks and spending hours at a Christian entertainment experience, any different than rocking out to the Rolling Stones, if it does not genuinely confront our hearts with the reality of God's presence, or require more of us as believers?

Are we distracted? Or are we disciples?

We have, wittingly or not, been pulled into the distractions of pop culture, and our ears are deaf to what is really important—especially the voice of Mordecai, pleading for our attention.

DISTRACTION IN THE CHURCH

When Jesus commissioned His early followers, He told them to "make disciples of all the nations" (Matt. 28:19).

Discipleship is not the transference of information, but the impartation of a new way of being. This necessitates modeling a lifestyle. There are absolutely no shortcuts in discipleship. You can't "hurry up" discipleship anymore than you can "hurry up" the growth of a tree. Discipleship does not happen from a pulpit. It happens over a cup of coffee, or at an outreach among the homeless, or in a late-night crisis prayer session, or while taking a few teenagers on a nature hike.

But somehow, in much of the Western Church, it seems that we have unknowingly adopted a state of corporate distraction that is almost totally hindering us from carrying out the commands of Scripture, such as in First Peter 1:22, which commands us to "love one another fervently with a pure heart."

Consider modern culture's state of distraction evidenced by the widespread pervasiveness of MySpace and similar online chat forums in daily life. This technology may be helpful to keep in touch with others, but if you look at our preoccupation with how many online "friends" we have, in comparison with the type of covenant friendship that David and Jonathan had in First Samuel 20 (which endangered both their lives), it becomes clear how we have lost sight of the principle of laying down our lives for others. We may know many more people, but our relationships are far more shallow.

Or take the reality television shows that appeal to the basest form of human nature. When participants in survival contests knowingly lose all human dignity and decency just to win fame and fortune, performing grotesque activities that are often utterly humiliating, I wonder how many steps away we are from the early Roman world that included the "sport" of watching animals tear apart human beings in the deadly Coliseum. What is happening to our testimony as salt and light to the world around us if we fill ourselves with the same mindlessness as the unredeemed?

Sadly, true discipleship has largely disappeared from our lifestyles, in favor of superficial relationships and religious programs that in themselves are oftentimes more a distraction from spiritual growth than a life-giving endeavor. Dan Juster says, "We have replaced genuine covenantal community and discipleship, and become giant religious event manufacturing organizations."[5]

The question remains: are we challenging each other to growth in true character and holiness, or are we settling for lukewarm, cultural norms?

The Western Church has so much to learn from our brothers and sisters around the world.

In May 2008 I had the opportunity to minister in Porto Seguro, Brazil, a guest of Apostle Rene TerraNova, at a nationwide conference of over 25,000 pastors and their families. What I saw there struck me powerfully. At the services I led, there was an incredible sense of the presence of God and the unity of those present. There was a "breakthrough" in the atmosphere that I can honestly say I have experienced few times elsewhere.

As I ask myself why that was, I can't forget how the spiritual atmosphere was completely independent of the natural surroundings we found ourselves in. The conference was held outdoors in a humid, 90-plus degree tent with services that ran for six to eight hours without so much as a bathroom break. Many did not even have chairs. The morning service began at 8:00 A.M. and went to 2:00 P.M. The people reassembled at 6:00 P.M. and the service went on to at least 1:00 A.M., often much later.

Even in these conditions, the times of corporate intercession, praying for one another, and crying-out prayer continued for hours, with little to no prompting from leaders for them to "keep pressing in." The Brazilians had learned the secret of tapping into a supernatural power that not only ushered in the miraculous but *disciplined their minds* for Kingdom productivity. Is there any wonder why astounding, weighty revelations and miraculous signs and wonders followed? They weren't distracted! They were there for God. They were there for His presence. His purpose. And one another. They were waiting on God. Waiting. The word itself implies the "sacrifice" of time. They were waiting, and God met them.

I also notice something about other traditions as I ponder this issue. In my grandmother's Catholic church, very little if anything has changed in their services over the past 50 years. When I attend services with her a few times a year and hear the Apostles' Creed and see the lit candles, and experience the liturgy of the service, there is something simple and focused and clear about their worship. The church service is not competing for my attention simply because it does not ever purport to *compete* with culture, but rather, to *speak to* culture. And amazingly, the attendance at her church has not really wavered over the years. It is steady because people are not there to be wowed by a performance. They are there for something they can't get from the distractions of this current age. They are there to engage their minds and hearts and to participate in something Holy, something "other."

Our fellowship as believers must go deeper than merely attending weekly services in which we stare at the back of someone's head for 90 minutes. This is not biblical fellowship. And for leaders, we must move beyond the place of polite collegiality at our monthly pastors meetings. We must advance to the level of *functional unity*, which means we will have to get real with one another. It is time for change to begin in the Household of God! This change can only come through a people who are committed to getting free of meaningless formalities and entering into life-giving relationships and enduring fruit.

I often say that disillusionment is a good thing because it implies that you must have been "illusioned" to begin with. *Get disillusioned.* Recognize the places where you may be stopping short of the deep, fulfilling relationship you truly desire with God and with other believers. I encourage you to examine your level of attachment to our entertainment culture, be it worldly entertainment, or the "spiritual" entertainment, which too often masks itself as worship, and make radical changes as the Holy Spirit directs.

GET DISILLUSIONED!

If you begin to take steps of obedience today, God will open up new realms of the Kingdom—delivering you from the power of distraction, releasing new focus into your daily life, and bringing you into His dynamic purpose.

Esther had to overcome the inner distractions of her insecurities and self-doubt, and the outer distractions of her lavish environment. If we are to accomplish the vital mission we have been charged with, we must do the same.

ENDNOTES

1. http://freedomkeys.com/quotations.htm.

2. http://www.internetworldstats.com/stats.htm.

3. Entertainment Trends, Plunkett Research; http://www.plunkettresearch.com/Industries/EntertainmentMedia/EntertainmentMediaStatistics/tabid/227/Default.aspx; accessed 6/9/08.

4. http://www.usatoday.com/life/television/news/2006-09-21-homes-tv_xhtm.

5. Dan Juster, director of Tikkun International, www.tikkunministries.org; personal reference.

~

CHAPTER 4

THE MALIGNANCY OF DENIAL

To run away from danger, instead of facing it,
is to deny one's faith in man and God,
even one's own self. It were better for
one to drown oneself than live to
declare such bankruptcy of faith.
—Mahatma Gandhi, November 24, 1946

De-ni-al: the psychological defense mechanism in which confrontation with a personal problem or with reality is avoided by
denying the existence of the problem or reality.

In other words: "Let's just pretend that everything is OK."

It's a common response. Everything from gaining weight to
the collapse of huge investment banks can happen (and be
hastened) because we like to live in a "propped up" reality; one
where facts matter less than feelings and public relations
advertising campaigns. We want things to be nice and to be good
and to work out like we see on television, because, after all, we're
not only Americans, we're Christians, and Jesus came to give us
a good life, didn't He?

While Esther enjoyed all of the extravagant distractions that
her relationship with the King afforded her, feeling more and

more secure, safe, and cared for by the minute, Haman was plotting the extermination of the Jews.

Then Haman said to King Ahasuerus, "There is a certain people scattered and dispersed among the people in all the provinces of your kingdom; their laws are different from all other people's, and they do not keep the king's laws. Therefore it is not fitting for the king to let them remain. If it pleases the king, let a decree be written that they be destroyed, and I will pay ten thousand talents of silver into the hands of those who do the work, to bring it into the king's treasuries." So the king took his signet ring from his hand and gave it to Haman, the son of Hammedatha the Agagite, the enemy of the Jews. And the king said to Haman, "The money and the people are given to you, to do with them as seems good to you." Then the king's scribes were called on the thirteenth day of the first month, and a decree was written according to all that Haman commanded—to the king's satraps, to the governors who were over each province, to the officials of all people, to every province according to its script, and to every people in their language. In the name of King Ahasuerus it was written, and sealed with the king's signet ring. And the letters were sent by couriers into all the king's provinces, to destroy, to kill, and to annihilate all the Jews, both young and old, little children and women, in one day, on the thirteenth day of the twelfth month, which is the month of Adar, and to plunder their possessions. A copy of the document was to be issued as law in every province, being published for all people, that they should be ready for that day. The couriers went out, hastened by the king's command; and the decree was proclaimed in Shushan the citadel. So the king and Haman sat down to drink, but the city of Shushan was perplexed (Esther 3:8-15).

It is interesting to note the story of Esther is one of the earliest recorded instances of national anti-Semitism, since the narrative far pre-dates Christianity. Certainly much, and perhaps most, anti-Semitism in the past 2,000 years has happened either at the hands of "Christians," or at least in the greater social context of Christendom, the horrific climax of this being, of course, the most unspeakable blight of darkness upon the human soul, the Holocaust, happening in the context of Christian Europe as the Church sat by, largely silent, and in denial.

The story of Esther proves that the enemy's vendetta against the children of Abraham is rooted in something much more primal than misguided religious aggression. There is something in the nature of Jewish existence itself, something in the fact that they, the Jews, even in exile, even far from faith, carry the testimony of the One True God with them by virtue of their very being, which causes satan to hate them (and those aligned with them) with a vengeance.

So Haman gains the complicit participation of the king, and begins preparing for the annihilation of the Jews, and Mordecai immediately reaches out to Esther with a warning. And do you remember Esther's reply? She says, in essence, "Mordecai, I cannot get involved...the King has not sent for me, and it could put me in a dangerous situation" (see Esther 4:11). Esther goes into a classic state of denial.

Esther had been told to deny, or at least to hide, her Jewish identity. And now, she finds denial a convenient way of dealing with unsettling information. Like the frog in the kettle, the heat rising around her, she does not move, thinking, *It can't be **that** bad*.

Esther is comfortable in the palace. She doesn't want to think about difficult things. The Jews in Susa, now in a state of shock and bewilderment (see Esther 3:15 NIV), seem very far away from the security she feels as she is surrounded by caring handmaidens, guardian eunuchs, and enjoying the prosperity and favor of the king. After all, isn't this the blessing of God? Isn't she enjoying the blessings she has hoped for from God?

Surely someone else will take care of that Haman situation. Surely somehow things will work themselves out...

PERFECTING THE ART OF DENIAL

Denial is a defense mechanism that has spread like a cancer throughout nations as well as the Christian Church. We tell ourselves, *I don't believe that is really happening, so it must not be real.* Or, *I don't understand what's going on, so it must not be true. I don't think that could really happen, so I'm just going to forget about it.* Scarlett O'Hara in the classic movie *Gone With the Wind* summed it up famously. Whenever she was confronted with anything difficult, her response invariably was, "I'll think about that tomorrow."[1]

Denial

When Esther was being pampered and primped, it was easy for her to deny the fact that Uncle Mordecai was trying to get a message through to her. It was easy to ignore someone who was trying to prick and pry her out of a comfortable place. Why did he want to bother her with warnings that may or may not be true? She was too comfortable in her new palatial surroundings to hear, or want to hear, anything but good news. She didn't want to deal with the fact that war had been declared on her and her people. She finally felt secure. She finally felt safe.

Like Esther, the American Church is all too often too comfortable in our blessed surroundings and we want to hear only good reports. We don't like the intensity of what we hear about all that "spiritual warfare." It sounds too radical, too extreme. The reality is, however, that it is not just spiritual warfare we are dealing with anymore. Now we're in a literal war. The conflicts we are fighting with actual weapons around the world are a manifestation of a spiritual battle taking place in the heavenlies. The spirit of Haman, the spirit of Hitler is alive and active in our day, and mobilizing with focus and determination to wipe out Israel and the West. And we, lulled into denial by our materialism and secularism, our televisions and our iPods, may have lost the spiritual backbone necessary to resist the invasion.

> # WE, LULLED INTO DENIAL BY OUR MATERIALISM AND
> ~ SECULARISM, MAY HAVE LOST ~
> THE SPIRITUAL BACKBONE NECESSARY TO RESIST THE INVASION.

Hear the cry of Mordecai as you read these recent words from Israeli government leader Benjamin Netanyahu.

> Now [we need] something that is particularly difficult. It requires what I call pre-emptive leadership. And of all the activities required in the political, economic and military fields, pre-emption is the most difficult. You can never prove to people what the situation would be if you do not move....

> All leadership exacts a cost—because otherwise you don't need leaders. You just need managers...you just run to the head of the herd. As it charges in one direction, you just charge along with it.

> Today what is required is leadership, leadership to change this tide of history, leadership to confront this danger—leadership to act....

> For us the Jewish people, too many times in our history we didn't see danger in time, and when we did, it was too late. Well, we see it now.... But can the world wake up? Can we wake up the world? Can we get the United States to act on its commitment—a commitment made by President Bush—he said we will not let Iran arm itself with nuclear weapons? Everybody in his right mind should support that position. It should be carried out. Can we get the world to do that?

A man I very much admire—he said "no." This is what *Winston Churchill* said in the House of Commons in 1935, about this tendency of democracies to sleep, while dangers lurk and gather up:

"There is nothing new in the story. It is as old as Rome. It falls into that long, dismal category of *the fruitlessness of experience* and the confirmed *unteachability of mankind*. Want of foresight, unwillingness to act when action would be simple and effective, lack of clear thinking, *confusion of counsel until the emergency comes*, until self-preservation strikes its jarring gong, these are the features which constitute *the endless repetition of history*."

So where are we in this? Do we get it? Does the world get it? Do they think it will pass? We're overstating it? *We're not.* It's 1938, Iran is Germany, and it is racing to acquire nuclear weapons.[2]

How is it possible that we choose, time and time again, denial over reality? How is it possible, as Churchill states, that that which is so clearly and obviously taught to us by history is ignored, and the pattern played out over and over again? Why do humans, individually and corporately, choose the comfort of a temporary lie rather than facing, with courage, the truth? I suggest several reasons why we run to denial rather than face reality.

FEARFULNESS

First and foremost, I think it is because we are afraid. Fear is a powerful motivator and can produce powerful reactions.

Do you remember when you were a child and something in your room frightened you? What did you do? You pulled the covers over your head. Nothing outside had changed a bit—everything that was (or wasn't) there was the same—but you felt safer because you were cocooned, unable to see what was scaring you.

For Esther to genuinely stare in the face of Haman's plot would have been a very scary thing for this young woman. For us to genuinely look at the reality of the plans of modern day Ahmadinejad, Osama bin Laden, and other Islamic warlords is a terrifying thing. Isn't that what we elect politicians for? They will handle it, we tell ourselves, as we pull our covers over our heads and go back to sleep.

But mother was right when she warned us that what we don't know can (and indeed most times *does*) hurt us. We may have good cause in natural terms to be very afraid, but fear is not just the opposite of courage; it is also the reason for it. As the oft-quoted maxim reminds us, "Courage is not the absence of fear but rather the judgment that something is more important than fear. The brave may not live forever, but the cautious do not live at all."[3]

~ FEAR IS NOT JUST THE OPPOSITE OF COURAGE; IT IS ALSO THE REASON FOR IT. ~

Esther needed only to recall the covenant of promise God made with her Father Abraham and his descendants to see there were more reasons for faith than for fear. "I will make you a great nation...I will bless those who bless you, and I will curse him who curses you" (Gen. 12:2-3).

By faith we are the inheritors of that same blessing, which is why we are exhorted to remember, "*God has not given us a spirit of fear, but of power and of love and of a sound mind*" 2 Tim. 1:7) and "*He who is in you is greater than he who is in the world*" (1 John 4:4b).

Like Elisha's servant Gehazi in Second Kings 6, we need to have our eyes opened to see the army of God that is on our side:

And when the servant of the man of God arose early and went out, there was an army, surrounding the city with horses and chariots. And his servant said to him, "Alas, my master! What shall we do?" So he answered, "Do not fear, for those who are with us are more than those who are with them." And Elisha prayed, and said, "Lord, I pray, open his eyes that he may see." Then the Lord opened the eyes of the young man, and he saw. And behold, the mountain was full of horses and chariots of fire all around Elisha (2 Kings 6:15-17).

Like Esther, we don't need to fear, but we do need to act.

SELFISHNESS

Another reason we embrace the false, temporary reality that denial offers us is that, fundamentally, we are creatures of habit, and we are selfish. To choose reality over denial means, very likely, that we will then need to do something about the reality we have seen. Inherent within the acceptance of reality is a call to action, a call to take responsibility for what we have now come to realize.

But that means readjusting priorities. That means our time and our money need to be spent differently. Our daily drifting toward leisure will need to be replaced with focused, decisive action. Parties may need to be replaced with prayer meetings. Trips to Hawaii with trips to Israel. Familiar Sunday school lessons on topics like "The Fruit of the Spirit" or "The Beatitudes" replaced with controversial ones like an analysis of the Middle East. It means writing letters to the editor and making phone calls to your legislators instead of watching television. It means being more courageous and confrontational in our day-to-day conversations. It means people might not like you.

PARTIES MAY NEED TO BE REPLACED WITH PRAYER MEET-INGS...TRIPS TO HAWAII WITH TRIPS TO ISRAEL.

I don't know of a better film depiction of reality vs. denial than the all-time hit movie *The Matrix*. In it, a small group of people become aware that some extremely advanced computers have found a way to completely take over the human race, and are now holding it in an artificial reality. The humans are completely unaware of this, however, because their captors, the computers, have programmed the minds of the captive humans and are feeding synthetic emotions and experiences into their brains to simulate "life as usual." A handful of humans escape this captive "matrix" and begin their fight to free the human race from the captivity that they are not even aware they are in.

One of the free humans, however, grows weary in the battle. They have no food, they are exhausted, they are constantly being chased by the machines, the battle seems destined to be lost, and he is ready to give up.

In the movie he goes to the enemy, the computer, and asks to be "plugged back in," really, to the ultimate place of denial. He knows he is asking to go back to a place that is completely unreal, but the pain and weariness of the battle he is fighting in the real world has completely worn him out, and he just doesn't care anymore. He explains to the computer, his enemy, that he would prefer a comfortable false reality to the strenuous, unpleasant existence of being truly alive.

The computer treats him to a "steak dinner," which is actually a computer simulation, and not real at all, but seems completely real to him because of how they are stimulating his brain. The character reveals his choice to enter into denial:

> "You know, I know this steak doesn't exist. I know that when I put it in my mouth, the Matrix is telling my brain…that it is juicy…and delicious. (He sighs.) After nine years [of fighting], you know what I realize? (He puts the bite of steak into his mouth, and sighs, as he chews it with his eyes closed.) Ignorance is bliss."[4]

It is hard to escape denial and embrace the reality that is here and swiftly approaching. Embracing reality places on you and me an inescapable responsibility to fight. It reorders our priorities and wreaks havoc to our comfort zones. But at the end of the day, truth is still the requisite for freedom (see John 8:32).

DECEPTION

When we add the understandable reaction of fear with the knee-jerk reaction of denial, they add up to a deadly combination:

Deception

Deception and denial are similar in many ways; but there are some slight but fundamental differences between the two that we must understand.

Denial is a reactive position we take to news that we don't want to acknowledge. I think of the defense mechanism of denial as a "quick shove"—pushing aside truth that is inconvenient and unwanted.

But when problems don't go away or improve, and indeed continue increasingly to present themselves to our consciousness, if we continue in denial, then we not only reactively ignore reality, but we must then proactively (even if subconsciously) begin creating a new reality based not on truth, but on lies.

In other words, if denial is a momentary, unthinking refusal of the truth, then deception is a long-term prison that we can subconsciously but intentionally begin to build for ourselves by refusing to walk in the light of truth. The apostle Paul refers to this idea in the Book of Romans.

> *For since the creation of the world His invisible attributes are clearly seen, being understood by the things that are made, even His eternal power and Godhead, so that they are without excuse, because, although they knew God, they did not glorify Him as God, nor were thankful, but became futile in their thoughts, and their foolish hearts were darkened. Professing to be wise, they became fools...* (Romans 1:20-22).

The Bible teaches us here that God has made truth pretty plain and simple. But when we are not willing to acknowledge Truth and its Source, there is a three-step process that ensues.

1. We become "vain in our imaginations"—in other words, we open our minds to a myriad of thoughts that are not grounded in truth. Thoughts and ideas flit and float without being challenged with the litmus test of truth.

2. Our hearts become "darkened." The cycle tightens in upon itself. The judgment inherent in not receiving and walking in light is that we will receive even less light than we currently have.

3. We end up as fools. Disconnected from God, from truth, from reality itself, we become the emperor of our own mind, strutting about in our "new clothes," and propped up in our false beliefs by those who are just as warped, scared, and deluded as we are.

~ DENIAL IS A DANGEROUS AND COSTLY DELAY OF THE INEVITABLE. ~

THE SCOURGE OF DENIAL

Esther heard Mordecai's warning, but her initial, knee-jerk reaction was to deny any level of responsibility she held in the matter. Let me remind you of the scene:

> *So Hathach returned and told Esther the words of Morde-cai. Then Esther spoke to Hathach, and gave him a com-mand for Mordecai: "All the king's servants and the people of the king's provinces know that any man or woman who goes into the inner court to the king, who has not been called, he has but one law: put all to death, except the one to whom the king holds out the golden scepter, that he may live. Yet I myself have not been called to go in to the king these thirty days"* (Esther 4:9-11).

In other words, "Mordecai, I hear what you're saying, but I cannot get involved. It could put my life in danger." And, in classic denial, Esther refused to understand that her life, and the life of all of her people, was already in grave danger.

And so today, if we the Church are the bride of the Great King, and if we are in the palace of His favor, what is our response to Mordecai's unsettling message? What is really happening in the American Christian Church, and the Church of the Western world?

Gene Edward Veith, in his article "Change-seekers: Survey reveals a nation on the spiritual hunt," makes an insightful statement when he says, "Despite the church growth movement and the proliferation of megachurches, evangelical Christianity is losing ground. ...Honestly facing the problem might bring American Christianity to a spiritual maturity that could reverse the slide."[5]

Notice the language? "Honestly facing the problem." Not denying it—but facing it head on.

For the United Kingdom, many are hypothesizing that it may be too late. According to Bishop Michael Nazir-Ali, radical Islam is filling a void created by the decline of Christianity. He claims that the social and sexual revolution of the 1960s had led to a steep decline in the influence of Christianity over society, a change which church leaders had failed to resist.

"It is this situation that has created the moral and spiritual vacuum in which we now find ourselves. While the Christian consensus was dissolved, nothing else, except perhaps endless self-indulgence, was put in its place," Bishop Nazir-Ali said in an interview in May 2008. The bishop, who faced death threats when he said that parts of Britain had become "no-go areas" for non-Muslims, said, "We are now confronted by another equally serious ideology, that of radical Islamism, which also claims to be comprehensive in scope. The consequences of the loss of this discourse are there for all to see: the destruction of the family because of the alleged parity of different forms of life together; the loss of a father figure, especially for boys, because the role of fathers is deemed otiose; the abuse of substances (including alcohol); the loss of respect for the human person leading to horrendous and mindless attacks on people."[6]

This situation in Great Britain was underscored when the Archbishop of Canterbury made the unbelievable statement that Christian England, the land of Whitefield and Wesley and Spurgeon, may soon need to accept the reality of Islamic Shari'ah law.

How long before it is too late for the United States? We choose to deny that Christian virtues of reverence, servant-hood, and reliability are being replaced with self-gratification and me-first attitudes. Our denial of what is going on in the Church (or perhaps more accurately, of what is *not* going on in the Church) and our refusal to bring about change is creating a vicious cycle. The less we take responsibility for establishing a godly reality, the more the enemies of Truth move in to define it for us.

THE LESS WE TAKE RESPONSIBILITY FOR ESTABLISHING A GODLY REALITY, THE MORE THE ENEMIES OF TRUTH MOVE IN TO DEFINE IT FOR US.

~

~

The sad truth in Esther's day, in Hitler's Germany, and in our day, is that evil does exist, and evil does advance where it is not confronted and disarmed.

Now, 70 years after Hitler's boasts were ignored and the Jewish people in particular and the world as a whole paid a huge price, today's Hamans are broadcasting their boasts, threatening the free world with the extinction of all that would stand in the way of their vision of the world united under radicalized Islam.

Today, one generation after our parents and grandparents fought and died in a world war so that we could continue enjoying a democracy that grants us freedom of religion, we are sacrificing our freedoms on the altar of our own apathy.

Esther did not want to think about the urgent threat of Haman. It was easier to forget it.

Chamberlain did not want to acknowledge Hitler's avowed dedication to the complete conquest of Europe. It was easier to appease it.

The Church in Europe did not want to get involved in a political affair that seemed "unspiritual" or outside the arena of religious responsibility. It was easier to rationalize it.

Many Jews in Germany and Europe did not want to acknowledge the rise of anti-Semitism surrounding them, even when it became violent. It was easier to ignore it.

It was easier to deny it—until it could no longer be denied.

And then it was too late.

ENDNOTES

1. *Gone With the Wind* (1939), directed by Victor Fleming, DVD edition.

2. Speech by Benjamin Netanyahu to United Jewish Communities General Assembly, Nov. 13, 2006, excerpt transcribed at http://jpundit.typepad.com /jci/2006/11/netanyahus_1938.html; accessed 8/29/08.

3. http://www.quoteland.com/search.asp; accessed 9/1/08.

4. *The Matrix* (1999), Warner Brothers, directed by Laurence and Andrew Wachowski, DVD edition.

5. Gene Edward Veith, "Change-seekers: Survey reveals a nation on the spiritual hunt," April 5/12, 2008, *World* magazine. Also see: "U.S. Religious Landscape Survey"; .http://religions.pewforum.org/reports; accessed 6/15/08.

6. Martin Beckford, "Bishop Michael Nazir-Ali: Radical Islam is filling void left by collapse of Christianity in UK," Telegraph.co.uk; 5/29/08; http://www.telegraph. co.uk/news/uknews/2042169/bishop; accessed 5/29/08.

CHAPTER 5

~

THE CRY OF MORDECAI

Ten people who speak make more noise
than ten thousand who are silent.[1]
—Napoleon

There was someone in Esther's life who was *not* ignoring the urgency of the moment. Someone who was fully alert to the coming destruction, and resolutely committed to doing all in his power to stop it. He was an interrupting voice, clearly discerning the situation, and he became a trumpet to rouse Esther to action.

It is often noted that the Book of Esther does not contain even one mention of God. God—His presence, miracles, angelic messengers, and supernatural wonders are strangely absent from this most epic of tales. It seems odd that miracles are so present and angels so available in other stories that seem to have much lesser implications. Let's be real—what is at stake in this story is the entire survival of the Jewish people. It is not healing a leper or raising a dead child, important as those things may be.

What we are talking about is the survival or obliteration of an entire nation.

Where is God?

Where are His angels?

Where are His miracles?

Where is His voice from Heaven?

Could it be that God is trying to teach us a very important lesson? Could it be that He is calling us to realize that there are times when it is *Him* waiting for *us* to do and act and be and save?

God is very present in Esther's story, but only in unseen ways. He is present in helping Esther be the right age and in the right place at the right time so that she is chosen for the king's harem. He is present in giving her favor and wisdom. He is present in ordering events in such a way that the king is re-minded of Mordecai's faithfulness, much to Haman's chagrin (more about that in Chapter 11). God is there, but He is moving in ways that are *supernaturally natural*, relying on people to walk out His purpose.

God is also very present in the voice and person of Mordecai. In so many ways, really, Mordecai is the central figure of the story, though most of the modern-day focus celebrates Esther. But it is faithful Mordecai who righteously adopts his orphaned niece. Wise Mordecai who counsels and instructs Esther about how to conduct herself. Righteous Mordecai who refuses to bow in worship to a man. Mordecai is somehow always on stage, but never center stage. Always present, but never dominant.

Without Mordecai, however, there would be no Esther. His penetrating, persistent, unrelenting voice called her to be more than she thought she could be; dared her to recognize the reality of her situation, and to act with holy boldness.

MORDECAI'S PENETRATING, PERSISTENT, UNRELENTING VOICE CALLED HER TO BE MORE THAN SHE THOUGHT SHE COULD BE.

Mordecai, I believe, is a picture of the Holy Spirit, the Inner Witness and Guide and Comforter of our hearts. He is a Father to the Fatherless and the Wonderful Counselor—the one who sticks closer than a brother. Each of us, when we turn to God, can experience the awakening sound of His voice, His guidance in our hearts. In a very real way, Mordecai became the voice of the Holy Spirit to Esther, hovering and watching over her from her youngest days until now when he is desperately trying to get a word to her in the palace, and ironically having a hard time getting through.

How easy it is to rely on the Holy Spirit when we are painfully aware of our lack and our need. How quickly we run to Him for solace, hope, and enrichment. But how quickly His tender voice is lost in the fray once His counsel leads us to the land of blessing. This is the test that Esther faces, and this is the test we face. Can we still hear Mordecai's voice through the thick palace walls of success?

Can His voice pierce the comfort zone that His caring guidance led us into? Will we remember our Guardian, our Counselor, or does His advice somehow now seem juvenile and unsophisticated? Is He a voice from our past to be tolerated with sweet remembrance, but not taken to heart anymore?

Esther faced the test of whether she would hear and heed Mordecai's cry. But Mordecai also faced a test, of whether he could speak out loud enough, strong enough, clear enough, and long enough to be heard. Other Mordecais have faced this same test.

WINSTON CHURCHILL

Like Mordecai, no one would listen to Winston Churchill's warnings of the folly of appeasing Hitler. Rather, he was called a warmonger and the opposition political party was forever throwing insults and mockery his way. Churchill felt it a necessity to bring together a Grand Alliance against the aggressor powers before it was too late. Churchill tried to rally others, but Neville Chamberlain's appeasement was forwarded as the way to deal with Hitler.

Regrettably, it was only after the first wave of German military power conquered Poland (then northwestern Europe, followed shortly by the fall of France) that, as one commentator wrote: "Churchill was called to supreme power and responsibility by a spontaneous revolt. He, almost alone of the nation's political leaders, was chosen by the will of the nation. For the next five years, perhaps the most heroic period in Britain's history, he held supreme command, as prime minister and minister of defense, in the nation's war effort. At this point his life and career became one with Britain's story and its survival."[2]

Churchill had to speak the truth about the dire circumstances facing Europe. Upon becoming prime minister he said: "I have nothing to offer but blood, toil, tears, and sweat: You ask, what is our policy? I will say: It is to wage war, by sea, land, and air, with all our might. You ask, what is our aim? I can answer in one word: Victory."[3]

Churchill broke through the distractions and denials surrounding the political arena in the United States to form an alliance with President Franklin D. Roosevelt. Fortunately, Roosevelt eventually heard the cry of the modern Mordecai (Churchill) and responded with military aid.

When Japan attacked Pearl Harbor in 1941, the United States knew it had to respond. Hitler then made the mistake of declaring war on the United States. Churchill's unforgettable speech to Congress after the Pearl Harbor attack expressed the inspiration and high resolve in the face of mortal danger that he had given his own patriots while they had fought alone for more than a year.

The Grand Alliance to combat aggression that Churchill had been trying to form since the 1930s was now a reality. Not until the summer of 1944 were the preparations complete for the invasion of Normandy, to break open Hitler's Europe. Churchill was so given to the effort as prime minister that he would have personally landed himself with the Allied forces on D-Day, but King George VI gave a direct order to prevent it.[4]

How would the war have been different, what could the outcome have been and how many precious lives would have been saved if Churchill had been listened to earlier? Similarly, imagine how much more horrible the outcome would have been, how unthinkable, if Churchill had given up and allowed discouragement and ridicule to silence him. He knew he had an alarm to trumpet and he knew everything depended on it, and so he did not give up.

~ CHURCHILL KNEW HE HAD AN ALARM TO TRUMPET AND HE KNEW EVERYTHING DEPENDED ON IT. ~

The last year of the war saw the famous partnership between Churchill and Roosevelt dissolving. In his famous "iron curtain" speech in the United States, he once again warned the West against Russia's aims and the aggrandizement of communism, making a plea for cooperation between the English-speaking peoples as the only hope of checking it. His warning was controversial, but events soon confirmed that Churchill's assessment was correct. Not until 1987 did the Cold War warm and communism fall, 42 years and eight U.S. presidents later.

Dietrich Bonhoeffer

Dietrich Bonhoeffer, a German pastor, played a significant role in the movement against Nazism in Germany in the 1930s. In 1934, 2,000 Lutheran pastors organized the Pastors' Emergency League in opposition to the state Church, which was controlled by the Nazis. This organization evolved into the Confessing Church, a free and independent Protestant Church, of which Bonhoeffer was a leader. The anti-Nazi activities of the Confessing Church were outlawed and its five seminaries closed by the Nazis in 1937.

Speaking out—trying to get the message to someone who could avert disaster—was unsuccessful. Bonhoeffer would urge people to reject the Nazi claim that the Fuehrer and the state deserved allegiance above that owed to God. He adamantly condemned Nazi persecution of the Jews, urging the Christian Church to stand with the Jews against Nazi oppression. On trips abroad he tried to garner support for the German resistance, but politicians were preoccupied with their own agendas, and cared little for his desperate plight.

Bonhoeffer's active opposition to National Socialism escalated to the point that he became part of a resistance cell inside the German military intelligence. He took part in a conspiracy to kill Hitler which failed and he along with others were arrested, imprisoned, and eventually executed. In his book, *The Cost of Discipleship*, Bonhoeffer condemned "cheap grace," and extolled "costly grace"—grace that requires radical obedience, even the willingness to die for one's beliefs.[5] Bonhoeffer was a Mordecai to the world, especially to the Church, but his voice was not loud enough, or rather, the Church's ears were too dull of hearing to perceive the accuracy of what he was saying.

Stiff Odds

Like Churchill and Bonhoeffer, Mordecai was up against stiff odds when it came to penetrating his niece's comfort zone. Although his message was of utmost importance, he was having a hard time making Esther realize that she was the only person who could save her people from annihilation. First he had to disengage her self-defense mechanisms of distraction and denial. Then, he had to stress the ominous reality of her circumstances.

> *And I will pray the Father, and He will give you another Helper, that He may abide with you forever—the Spirit of truth, whom the world cannot receive, because it neither sees Him nor knows Him; but you know Him, for He dwells with you and will be in you.* ***I will not leave you orphans;*** *I will come to you* (John 14:16-18).

Mordecai came to his niece after her parents died. He comforted her, loved her, and raised her as best an uncle could. No doubt he protected her and provided for her. I'm sure that, over time, she came to trust him and deeply valued his advice. Yet sometime after she arguably became the most powerful woman in the known world, her response to Mordecai's voice became somewhat dulled, no doubt due to the complexity of her newfound life.

How often do you suppose the Holy Spirit tries to deliver a critical message to us, only to find us too distracted, too in denial to perceive His voice? How often do we refuse to acknowledge the still, small voice trying to get our attention?

On a broader scale, how many times have we read headlines that go against everything we believe in, and have quickly turned the page or changed the channel? How many times have we seen pictures of bombs exploding in places where terrorists know there are Jews and tourists, and felt no compassion? How many times have we heard about the fighting between Israelis and Palestinians, dismissing this as if it were reciprocal feuding between two equally-responsible parties rather than truly investigating the underlying causes for the continued upheaval? In every single decade of its existence, the state of Israel has been threatened or attacked militarily.

How could Esther not have realized that the survival of her people meant her own survival as well? How can we not realize that Israel's battle is our own, and that today, in a thousand ways, the Mordecai voice of the Holy Spirit is calling out to us to be an influence, to be an alarm, to be a force while we still have the chance?

∼ HOW COULD ESTHER NOT HAVE REALIZED THAT THE SURVIVAL OF HER PEOPLE MEANT HER OWN SURVIVAL AS WELL? ∼

Mordecai's message was not a comfortable one. It was not cheering, convenient, or easy to hear. In the same way, the voice of the Spirit speaking to His Church today is not usually popular. As indicated by Jesus Himself, His message is for those who have "ears to hear." Both then and now, it is common to hear words but not be moved by them.

ISRAEL—CRY OF THE SPIRIT

One of the chief ways the "Mordecai" voice of the Spirit is crying out to the "Esther" Church of today is through the prophetic picture of God's covenant land and people—Israel— through her birth, existence, and current struggles.

For so many of us, we perceive Israel as foreign, disconnected from us, both because we are Christians and because we are Western; and Israel is part of the Middle East. The Jews, by and large, have not accepted Jesus, and the secular State of Israel seems far away and very removed from our cultural milieu. These perceptions can cause us to feel detached from the land and the people God calls His own.

And yet we are those who are "grafted in" to the covenants of God with the Jewish people, by faith (see Rom. 11:18-20).

Paul clearly states that "God has not cast away His people [Israel] whom He foreknew" (Rom. 11:2a). And, if we truly believe that Jesus will return to the city of Jerusalem, then we certainly must have a sense of identification and concern for the place of His passion, His resurrection, and His Second Coming.

The re-gathering of the Jewish people to their ancestral homeland is one of the chief prophetic promises in all of Scripture. Dozens of times throughout the Old Testament, God declares that there will be a day when Israel is gathered from the nations back to her native soil.

Beloved, how much louder and more clearly could God speak than by—in our day, in front of the eyes of the nations, and out of the ashes of the Holocaust—bringing back His chosen people to their Promised Land? Is this not the voice of Mordecai crying to us today, "Be alert! Pay attention! You are living in prophetic times...you are part of a prophetic generation"?

~ HOW MUCH LOUDER AND MORE CLEARLY COULD GOD SPEAK THAN BY BRINGING BACK HIS CHOSEN PEOPLE TO THEIR PROMISED LAND? ~

When Esther arrived in the palace, she felt safe and secure. Her surroundings caused her to feel completely at ease. Likewise, the comfortable Church in the West (and particularly the United States) seems to have a presumptuous triumphalism affecting (or infecting) it; which is based on poor theology, historical ignorance, and further refutation or outright denial of the existential crisis regarding the future of Christianity in the face of jihadist Islam.

Proof texts such as "...I will build My church, and the gates of hell shall not prevail against it" (Matt. 16:18b ESV) are thrown about, as we seek to convince ourselves that America is for some reason immune to the persecution and martyrdom that is rapidly advancing toward us and is even now prevailing against our brethren worldwide through the sword of Islam. We fail to remember there are places where Christianity once flourished as the overwhelming majority (such as Turkey where the early apostles founded the seven churches mentioned in the Book of Revelation), but where today Islam is in complete ascendancy.

Biblically we know that there will always be a pure and indeed triumphant expression of His Church in the earth. This, however, is *His* Church, not *our* Church as we have designed and wanted her to be. It is not our cultural comfort zone that God has promised to preserve. God is not committed to preserving our religious programs or our big buildings. Rather, He has promised a day of reckoning.

IT IS NOT OUR CULTURAL COMFORT ZONE THAT GOD HAS PROMISED TO PRESERVE.

See that you do not refuse Him who speaks. For if they did not escape who refused Him who spoke on earth, much more shall we not escape if we turn away from Him who speaks from heaven, whose voice then shook the earth; but now He has promised, saying, "Yet once more I shake not only the earth, but also heaven." Now this, "Yet once more," indicates the removal of those things that are being shaken, as of things that are made, that the things which cannot be shaken may remain. Therefore, since we are receiving a kingdom which cannot be shaken, let us have grace, by which we may serve God acceptably with reverence and godly fear. For our God is a consuming fire (Hebrews 12:25-29).

Can you hear a Mordecai message for today within these verses?

"See that you do not refuse Him who speaks..." (Heb. 12:25a). Was this not the very thing that Esther was doing? She was refusing the voice of the one who had cared for her, provided for her, raised her. Now his voice was unsettling, disturbing, even radical in nature. Surely the old man was overreacting, surely things weren't all that bad!

God promises us that a time of shaking is coming...when everything that is not founded and built on the Rock will crumble. In order to fulfill her destiny, I believe the American Church has to awaken from the fairy tale that suggests "all's right with the world," and stand in the position she has been called to occupy in this hour. And for our battle plan, we must hear the Holy Spirit and look to Israel.

If Mordecai were alive today, I believe he would challenge us to contemplate these three areas in which the people of Israel are waging the front lines battle for faith, freedom, and the future of humankind.

1. Spiritually

Those who call themselves Christians and deny the Jewish people's place in God's heart are in for the rudest awakening. *To entertain the idea that God's covenant people are somehow now spiritually obsolete is erroneous at best and heretical at worst.*

God's covenantal mercies to us are simply a reflection and continuation of His covenant with Abraham, Isaac, and Jacob. And if God doesn't keep His covenant with Israel, what obligation would He have to keep covenant with us—the wild olive branch grafted into the root of their faith (see Rom. 11:17)?

Covenantal blessing equals covenantal responsibility.

~ COVENANTAL BLESSING EQUALS COVENANTAL RESPONSIBILITY. ~

It is imperative that everyone who has become part of God's enduring legacy of faithfulness to humanity honor those through whom He has shown Himself faithful. We know God because, through centuries of abject persecution, the Jewish people kept lighting the Sabbath candles week after week, keeping the flame of the Lord's presence alive in the earth.

We owe a debt to the Jewish people for maintaining, in exile after exile, their hope in the covenantal promises of God. We can express our gratitude and honor to them by loving, caring for, and standing with His children. Addressing this same issue, the Book of Romans instructs us, "…[I]f the Gentiles have shared in the Jews' spiritual blessings, they owe it to the Jews to share with them their material blessings" (Rom. 15:27 NIV).

Or consider this directive from the Book of Isaiah:

I have posted watchmen on your walls, O Jerusalem; they will never be silent day or night. You who call on the Lord, give yourselves no rest, and give him no rest till he establishes Jerusalem and makes her the praise of the earth (Isaiah 62:6-7 NIV).

Let me ask you this…Have you called on the name of the Lord? For healing, for counsel, for your very salvation? For those of us who have answered "yes" to any one of these questions, we have the obligation to also cry out to Him for the establishing of Jerusalem. The text does not say "You *Jews* who call on the Lord…" or "You who have a spiritual burden for Israel call on the Lord…."

No. *All* who call on the Lord must also seek the welfare of His city.

2. Physically

It is difficult for those in the West to imagine the kind of terror that pervades Israeli culture due to living under constant attack by Islamic extremists. Suffice it to say that those living in Israel do not have the luxury of divorcing spirituality from day-to-day life.

Put yourself in their shoes: You live in the Holy Land, but when you board the bus every morning, you have to hope that a militant suicide bomber has not chosen that bus, that morning, to gain his entrance to the supposed 70 virgins in paradise by blowing up Jews.

Several times I have had secular, non-religious Israelis confront me in conversation with a penetrating question that I have not yet been able to answer.

"Robert," they say, "Bethlehem, the birthplace of the one you call your Savior, was for 2,000 years a Christian city. We had safety and peace and cooperation with the Christians living in Bethlehem. Now, in just 10 years time, Bethlehem has shifted from being 90 percent Christian, to less than 10 percent Christian. Now, 90 percent or more of the city you call the birthplace of your faith has been given to the Muslims who have driven out the Christians through fear, intimidation, harassment, and often outright violence. And so now for us Israelis, the front lines of Islam are that much closer.

"How is it possible," they ask me, "that you Christians, after 2,000 years of celebrating Jesus' life in that city, care so little for His birthplace that you are willing to hand it over to the Muslims without giving it a second thought?"

And I have no answer for them. I don't know how it is possible. How is it that we have so completely divorced the spiritual from the natural; the "what we're willing to say" from the "what we're willing to do"? And if the Jewish people today are asking that question, wouldn't our Savior (a Jewish rabbi) be wondering the same thing?

HOW IS IT THAT WE HAVE SO COMPLETELY DIVORCED THE SPIRITUAL FROM THE NATURAL?

When will the front lines of the battle be close enough that it moves us to action? What more will we have to lose in order to realize what has already been taken from us? When will we understand that the "little town of Bethlehem" is not a Christmas carol, but a city besieged?

Israel equals reality. When we wrestle with the question and conundrum of Israel, the process confronts our unprovoked safety zones and demands a response. In Israel, spiritual beliefs cannot be separated from practical actions.

3. Ideologically

Whatever degree of safety we have in the United States against the rising tide of militant Islam, we owe in large part to the heroism of Israelis who live on the front lines of this existential battle for Western civilization. I am not only speaking in military terms. Israel's determination to remain a democracy in a sea of 22 hostile Islamic states—especially when demographically this causes her future to be endangered on a daily basis—is a massive demonstration of noble courage.

Israel, like any other nation, like the United States, is not perfect. She has her weaknesses as well as outright flaws. But there is no question that by any moral standard, she is unequivocally standing on the side of all that we call honorable. If you do not believe that, you are either uninformed or misinformed. There is also no doubt that by standing on the side of the right, Israel has become the wall of protection that is bearing the brunt of the growing jihadist attacks against our shared values and way of life. And yet it seems that much of the American Church (perhaps because of the aforementioned mindset of triumphalism) remains unmoved by and uninvolved in Israel's struggle. Instead, we choose to ignore the reality of the approaching danger (since you are driving to work instead of taking the bus in Israel, and since you most likely are not Jewish), and are content to let someone else— Israel—guard the wall, be the wall, that protects us.

The exceptions to this (such as the global Day of Prayer for the Peace of Jerusalem and Christians United for Israel) are not nearly enough of a response to the urgency of the hour. A nuclear Iran, led by a modern-day Hitler madman, and the bloodthirsty organizations of al-Qaeda, Hezbollah, and Hamas, who joyfully offer the blood sacrifice of their children to murder Israeli civilians, are just a few of the looming demonic powers arrayed against Israel (and you) at this moment.

I invite you today to hear Mordecai's cry *now*, rather than later; to realize that Israel's struggle is your struggle. Israel's cause is your cause. Israel's survival is your own. Begin to study and engage your mind, heart, and spirit. You will find your comfort melting away and your priorities changing. When you begin to wrestle with the questions of Israel, even as Israel of old once wrestled with God, things will happen in your life. You will, like Jacob, be changed by the process, and perhaps limp a little, but also receive a new, unshakable identity.

Move from the place of spectator to the place of the alert, awakened watchman on the wall. Hear the voice of the Comforter calling you to holy discomfort.

A PIERCING CRY

Crisis clarifies. Simply put, it is the only single thing I can think of that can bring an individual or a people to a place where they can see with absolute clarity and hear distinctly the Mordecais in their lives. Crisis brings clarity because it forces us to choose (and to act on) what we believe.

~ CRISIS BRINGS CLARITY BECAUSE IT FORCES US TO CHOOSE (AND TO ACT ON) WHAT WE BELIEVE. ~

When there is no threat—no present danger—we float along, content with the status quo. In this sort of climate, our senses grow dull and we lose that sense of purpose God implanted into all of us. My observation is that it usually takes some kind of calamity to snap people out of their stupor and bring them to a place where they can regain a sense of direction. The Church in the West, and particularly in the United States, is facing a crisis which, I believe, will call her to question who she is, what she believes, and where she will go in the days ahead.

We have the option of giving up. Or we could allow the crisis we see in our nation and the nations of the earth to move us to unshakable resolve, to believe the promises of God for us and for Israel and the nations, and from that place of faith, to overcome in the inevitable battle ahead.

If you are facing personal crisis, or if you are simply aware of the urgent state of affairs facing the people of God in this hour, I want to encourage you: *God is giving you the chance to participate in the greatest victory of all time!* If you choose to believe that the God of Israel will come out on top of every crisis, I am convinced that you will begin to, in faith, pray for the peace of Jerusalem as never before.

Allow Mordecai, the Holy Spirit, to penetrate your comfort zone with His counsel and His words of truth. In this hour of crisis, may you find yourself on the side that stands in faith, stands in prayer, and stands with the God of Israel.

ENDNOTES

1. http://freedomkeys.com/quotations.htm.
2. Winston Churchill; http://www.grolier.com/wwii/wwii _churchill.html; accessed 6/27/08.
3. Ibid.
4. Ibid.

5. Dietrich   Bonhoeffer;   http://www.iep.utm.edu/b
   /bonhoeff.htm; accessed 6/27/08. And http://www
   . p b s . o r g / w n e t / r e l i g i o n a n d e t h i c s / w e e k
   923/feature.html; accessed 6/27/08.

CHAPTER 6

~

ESTHER'S TRANSFORMATION

Everyone thinks of changing the world,
but no one thinks of changing himself.[1]
—Leo Tolstoy

Most of us remember the science class assignment from grade school of observing the metamorphosis of a caterpillar into a butterfly. Children rove the playground searching for caterpillars, bring them into the classroom, and carefully place them in an aquarium, feeding them leaves for the next several weeks. Eventually the fuzzy fellows cocoon themselves into tiny, inconspicuous bundles, and the waiting begins. One morning, you come into school to find the cocoons being hatched open, and bright, winged creatures emerging.

Transformation is a powerful phenomenon.

Can people really change? And if so, how? How do we really, fundamentally change as human beings? Are we forever locked into whatever patterns nature and nurture left us with in childhood? Or can we see a new reality created in our lives?

At this point, you may be thinking, *Why is he talking about transformation? What transformation did Esther undergo? She was beautiful to begin with! Sure, she soaked in oil and spices for a year, but let's face it, that was pretty much gilding the lily.*

Yes, but Esther's most profound transformation was not outward, but inward. It's not about what's happening on the surface, but rather what is beneath the surface that constitutes a genuine metamorphosis. From a subservient, intimidated orphan girl to engaging in political espionage to save her people from genocide, Esther transforms from insecure bride to strategic savior.

PERSIA'S SWEETHEART

As far as we can tell, Esther was a wise and good girl. We can see from her actions upon first being summoned to appear before the king that she had a measure of self-possession the other young women seemed to lack, and a strength of character that led her to remain true to herself despite all the intoxicating allurements of royal living. She was mature beyond her years and made choices that allowed her to excel beyond her competition at every turn. This was no doubt due to the quality upbringing she had received from her Uncle Mordecai.

I love the portrait Scripture paints of this relationship. There appears to be a bond between this distantly-related pair that not all parents share with even their natural-born children.

Scripture gives no indication that Mordecai had ever married, and so he likely would have been childless as well. When his relative died, leaving him a totally dependent charge, what might his reaction have been? Did he feel overwhelmed at the prospect of raising a child—much less a girl—on his own? Let's imagine…a gruff, wrinkly, proud old man who had never deeply loved another human being; and a young, helpless, dark-eyed little beauty who had no hope in the world but him. This unlikely pair was brought together by the Lord for divine purpose!

We can presume that Mordecai invested much of his energy and attention into "his" little girl. As he poured all the insight and paternal affection he had into this solitary little child, he watched her grow into a lovely young woman who captured the gaze of all who saw her—not only through her outer, but also her inner beauty.

How proud he must have been of his little Esther! The care with which he raised Esther did not fade as she matured. Scripture says that even after she had been taken into the palace, Mordecai "paced in front of the court of the women's quarters, to learn of Esther's welfare and what was happening to her" (Esther 2:11).

Yes, Mordecai had done well. He had raised a good girl—even the best—one could argue, in the entire Kingdom. She was so good, so obedient, in fact, that she followed her uncle's instruction even when she was out on her own. "Esther had not yet made known her kindred or her people, even as Mordecai had commanded her; for Esther did what Mordecai told her as she had done when under his care" (Esther 2:20 NASB).

This relationship, however, was about to be tested to the utmost.

Esther had, in the short years of her young life, achieved what few others, before or since, can lay claim to. She had made it to the top, and she had done so by doing everything right. There was no pettiness, no compromise, no backhanded deals that marred her legendary ascent to the pinnacle of favor upon which she now stood. She had listened. She had obeyed. She had done all that had ever been asked of her, and she did it with exceptional poise, grace, and honor. And at every turn, she had been rewarded in abundance by the God of Heaven, who seemed not to hold anything back of her every heart's desire. She turned the age-old maxim on its head by proving, "Nice girls finish first." Pretty *and* perfect, Esther seemed to have it all.

ESTHER HAD MADE IT TO THE TOP, AND SHE HAD DONE SO BY DOING EVERYTHING RIGHT.

Then at just the point Esther was no doubt about to finish perfecting perfection (as can happen too often in our lives when we finally think things are going well), something unforeseen, unprecedented, and extremely imperfect comes her way.

Esther learns of a plot that would destroy her people.

We know that Esther understood the severity of the threat because we are told that, upon hearing the report, "the queen writhed in great anguish" (Esther 4:4 NASB). But what is equally as obvious is that she did not want to deal with it. Instead of joining Mordecai by putting on sackcloth herself, she sends her uncle beautiful new garments to wear instead of his mourning attire. By this time Esther must have been accustomed to fine apparel. Did she think that a new outfit would make the bad news go away? That same defense mechanism of denial was still at work—shielding her from a reality she didn't want to confront.

Mordecai refuses the clothes, not allowing himself to be comforted by his niece's gesture. Esther then decides to investigate by sending someone to find out more from Mordecai, and receives the response she dreaded to hear. Her most cherished advisor, the only voice she had ever known and trusted, suggests to her that she go before the king to plead on behalf of her people.

What do we do when the trusted voice of the Spirit, who has led us by gentle paths and green pastures, suddenly calls us to the terrifying heights of the mountain, or the dense, dark, untraversed depths of the valley? What do you do when the steadfast voice of God all of a sudden doesn't make sense?

When the Voice that all along has kept you safe, now tells you to do something that seems nothing short of perilous?

∼ WHAT DO YOU DO WHEN THE STEADFAST VOICE OF GOD ALL OF A SUDDEN DOESN'T MAKE SENSE? ∼

Esther knew exactly what was being asked of her by Mordecai, and she knew (in her mind) exactly why it wouldn't work. When the idea was presented to her, she reminds him of the law, as if he didn't know it:

> *All the king's servants and the people of the king's provinces know that any man or woman who goes into the inner court to the king, who has not been called, he has but one law: put all to death, except the one to whom the king holds out the golden scepter, that he may live. Yet I myself have not been called to go in to the king these thirty days* (Esther 4:11).

Esther was a realist. She knew what her domain was and that her role in the king's life did not involve political consultation. Approaching the king in front of the royal court about revoking an ordinance advantageous to his treasury was not a smart move for her. This was not the bedroom, it was the throne room. Simply put, she was out of her league. Mordecai's counsel and guidance, for the first time, seemed unreasonable and unwise.

RISKY BUSINESS

For the first time, Esther, the "good girl," who had achieved success by listening to Mordecai, is in a quandary. The problem wasn't that she didn't want to do the right thing; the problem was that, this time, the right thing seemed so clearly to be the wrong thing, the unwise thing. This time, there was risk involved; this time, she had something to lose. After a lifetime of acing every test, winning every beauty pageant, and befriending all around her, Esther had to do a 180 and take the ultimate "unwise" step. All of this was exacerbated by one seemingly insignificant detail: Esther had never before broken the rules.

Everything Mordecai had told her to do up to this point had made sense. It made sense to keep her Jewish identity a secret, it made sense to behave with respectability and decorum among strangers. It made sense to take in with her to the king that first night only that which Hegai the eunuch (the man in the know) had advised.

It did not, however, in any way make sense to intentionally defy the law by going before the king, unsummoned and unannounced, to beseech him to annul an edict proposed by his highest ranking official, which he had already approved and which, he believed, would eliminate a threat to his kingdom. (Before you diminish the magnitude of this act, don't forget that the last queen had been banished for not observing palace protocol. This king had a habit of disposing of queens. Could it be that Esther, who had not been called on for the past 30 days, would end up like her predecessor?)

Esther was being asked to do something out of her realm of expertise—to take a complete leap of faith. She had no problem following sound instruction and doing that which would gain her the approval of everyone she knew. She didn't mind playing it safe. This had always worked for her. The formula for her life thus far had been a simple one: opportunity plus obedience equals blessing. But now the game was changing.

Doing the right thing now would require something Esther had never needed before—a will of her own.

A WILL OF ONE'S OWN

Everyone thinks Esther's big moment is when she comes before the king, unsummoned. But by that time, her fate was already well out of her hands. Esther's defining moment actually came before that, in front of a much smaller audience. Esther's defining moment was when she realized her story was not about her and her safety, but about her yielding her will and the position she had been given to a higher call, requiring her to risk everything. Esther says:

> *Go, gather all the Jews who are present in Shushan, and fast for me; neither eat nor drink for three days, night or day. My maids and I will fast likewise. And so I will go to the king, which is against the law; and if I perish, I perish!* (Esther 4:16)

> Have you ever read the story this way: "*I will* go to the king…" (vs. 16). The first words of that statement are apt to be ignored in light of the climactic "if I perish, I perish!" But what a world of commitment is contained in that "I will"! Rather big words for such a little girl, but Esther wasn't a little girl anymore. With her faith-filled, bold, and solemn vow, she left the world of beauty pageantry and successfully made the transition from good girl to *God's* girl.

By making this declaration, Esther agrees that her will is one with the will of the Father and the destiny He has ordained over her life. In that one moment, she becomes the heroine of her own story instead of the concubine in someone else's.

~ IN THAT ONE MOMENT SHE BECOMES THE HEROINE OF HER OWN STORY, INSTEAD OF THE CONCUBINE IN SOMEONE ELSE'S. ~

Because almost everyone reading this book has never known anything but a life of freedom, we all are guilty of taking the sovereignty we hold over ourselves, our ability to make so many choices, for granted. Because most of us have never lived under a tyrant master who dictated our every move, we don't know what it is to live without self-determination. Because of this we can easily go our whole lives without realizing that every step of the way we are guided by our own free will.

The power of choice, of free human will is an awesome thing. It pervades every aspect of our existence and can achieve, at times, even what the imagination cannot. This most essential of all human freedoms is the one thing that no matter how dire our circumstances may be, can never be taken away from us.

Viktor Frankl, an Austrian psychiatrist who was interned at a concentration camp by the Nazi regime during World War II, has a powerful testimony that illustrates this point exactly. After experiencing the unspeakable atrocities of the Holocaust, Frankl came to an important realization: no matter what was done to him, his oppressors could not take from him one seemingly small liberty: the ability to choose. Even though so many freedoms had been taken from him, he always had at least one, no matter how minuscule it was. Hidden at the core of his being lay the ability to choose his reaction to any and every situation.

Because he realized that no one could ever control him completely, he maintained the knowledge of who he really was. He never gave up his beliefs, and so was a source of hope, strength, and inspiration to his fellow prisoners.

One of the many insightful observations Frankl makes in the account he wrote of his experiences in the concentration camp, asserts, "When we are no longer able to change a situation…we are challenged to change ourselves."[2]

Esther, in herself, could not change the situation facing her people. She did not have that authority. But she could lay everything on the line and change herself from a frightened, passive bystander to an active, principal player.

When Frankl was released from the camp at the end of the war, he returned to his practice and went on to establish a psychotherapeutic movement called logotherapy, which teaches people how to respond to challenging situations with moral courage, by understanding that the purpose of their lives is being wrought in the midst of *whatever* they are facing.

The power to act is crucial. It didn't matter to Esther that her choice to go before the king would more than likely cause her head to end up on a block; that, she had no control over. But the choice to act *was* within her power, and so she did what she knew she must. She came to the conclusion that she would do this one thing, even if it was the last thing she ever did.

The wide-eyed little Esther who had come to the palace, no doubt dazzled by the glitz and glam of this new world, must have instantaneously seen all those jewels in a different light. Her too-good-to-be-true dream turned out to be just that, as she was slapped across the face with the reality of the enemy's cunning subterfuge. She was faced with a choice, and the choice was hers alone to make.

She had not seen her story told in flannelgraph figures in Sunday school or celebrated in Purim. She did not know how things would turn out. All she knew was that she had been chosen for a reason. She had been blessed for a purpose. She had come to royalty for such a time as this.

THE POINT OF NO RETURN

Did she have it in her? She had the looks of a movie star, a heart of obedience, but it remained to be seen whether or not Esther had what it took to single-handedly turn around an impending holocaust. She was a submissive niece, a fetching lover, but was she a fighter?

To act on Mordecai's request would take an extraordinary act of will; so much was at stake for the fledgling queen. Was she going to risk losing all the favor she had worked so hard to gain?

Esther's was, perhaps, the ultimate rags-to-riches saga. She rose out of obscurity and was transformed from orphan peasant to Persian queen. How's *that* for a happy ending? Didn't Esther have the right to live happily ever after? Esther, the outsider; Esther, the subjugated; Esther, the orphan. Fortune had finally smiled upon her. Surely Esther was entitled to a little something for herself.

∼ DIDN'T ESTHER HAVE THE RIGHT TO LIVE HAPPILY EVER AFTER? ∼

You can almost hear the thoughts racing through her mind when Mordecai first brings her word of the impending danger and her proposed role to intervene. *But Mordecai, this is how my story is supposed to end. This is where I belong. Me in the palace...me in the court...me in the arms of the King...me, me, me!*

But in so doing, she would have made the same mistake we all make when we commit the error of thinking for God: we think too small.

Of course we all know what Esther chose. We recall her famous line, in which she counted her life as nothing next to the imperative of speaking out for the welfare of her people. The question: what made Esther say yes? What made her lay everything on the line in hopes that her fragile life could overcome the evil assault that was arrayed against her?

Revisit this epic moment in the history of faith:

> And Mordecai told them to answer Esther: "Do not think in your heart that you will escape in the king's palace any more than all the other Jews. For if you remain completely silent at this time, relief and deliverance will arise for the Jews from another place, but you and your father's house will perish. Yet who knows whether you have come to the kingdom for such a time as this?"

> *Then Esther told them to reply to Mordecai: "Go, gather all the Jews who are present in Shushan, and fast for me; neither eat nor drink for three days, night or day. My maids and I will fast likewise. And so I will go to the king, which is against the law; and if I perish, I perish!"* (Esther 4:13-16)

Take notice of the so miniscule, yet ever-so-important space between the question mark of Mordecai's plea and the "Then" of Esther's reply. It is just a blank space…the space between Mordecai's plea and Esther's answer. But this blank space has become one of my favorite places in all of Scripture. Something powerful, something life-changing, something history-shaping took place between those two words.

Something turned in Esther's heart, and history turned with it.

∽ SOMETHING TURNED IN ESTHER'S HEART, AND HISTORY TURNED WITH IT. ∽

The Esther before that space and the Esther after are two completely different people.

Another version records Esther's decision in these frank and simple words: *"I will go to the king **even though** it is against the law…"* (Esther 4:16b NIV).

Esther had come to her first "even-though" moment in which she was faced with a decision between the easy or the difficult, the safe or the dangerous, the benign or the controversial. Even-though moments are those times when you know that you know that you know you must do what's right—*even though* the consequences may be very costly.

An even-though moment means that you must move from the sidelines to the playing field. From the darkness of backstage to the glare of the center stage spotlight. All eyes are on you and the pressure is on.

She could just as easily have said no. In fact, she could much *more* easily have said no. Not taking the easy way out pitted her against the law, against common sense, and against the second most powerful man in the entire empire. Everything was against her the moment she chose to speak out. Yet she boldly chose which side of "even though" she was going to stand on.

What brought on this inner transformation? We will never know. We are given no indication of what it was that caused her thought process to change. All we know is that the girl from Susa said yes, and because of that, the Jewish people are alive today.

The beginning of this chapter talked about the experience of transformation, and how the most authentic type of transformation is one that cannot be directly observed, but rather felt.

Esther made just such a transformation, and the world today is still talking about it.

Beloved, being a good, "safe" person may win you favor in the eyes of all who see you; it may even help you win the hearts of those in earthly authority, but simply being a good person, content to sit on the sidelines, never changed the course of human history. It takes something much more to accomplish that.

I believe there were five breakthroughs Esther experienced, which allowed her to respond rightly to her even-though moment. I have dedicated the next five chapters to looking at each of them in depth. My hope is that you will discover not only how Esther broke through to victory, but how you can do the same in the critical days in which we live.

ENDNOTES

1. http://www.quotegarden.com/helping.html.

2. Viktor E. Frankl, *Man's Search for Meaning* (Boston: Beacon Press, 2006 ed.), 112.

CHAPTER 7

~

BREAKTHROUGH #1—
RECOGNIZING REALITY

*We can evade reality, but we cannot
evade the consequences of evading reality.*[1]
—Ayn Rand

If you walk into any 12-step program meeting across the globe, you will encounter people who are actively attempting to deal with an issue in their lives by getting the help they need to bring about significant lifestyle changes. But when they walk through the door for the first time, they are not asked to come up with an elaborate 19-point plan on achieving their recovery. They are asked to take one initial step, without which it is impossible to progress on their journey. And as we all know by now, the first step in overcoming any personal obstacle is *admitting you have a problem.*

The first breakthrough Esther experienced was that of recognizing reality. This may sound too trivial to constitute a breakthrough, but I don't for a moment believe that it is. While there is ultimately only one true reality (that of the One, True

111

God), there seems to be no shortage of alternate realities one can choose to live under.

WHOSE REALITY?

Today, everyone, everywhere seems to be obsessed with reality. On one level this is quite commendable and I am completely in favor of living in openness with others. I have a growing conviction, however, that the only reality people really want to accept these days is the one they have created for themselves. From one reality television show to the next, our culture is floating along in a self-absorbed existence that has little to do with reality as God sees it, or honestly, the reality of the world outside of the Western hemisphere.

Esther might not have had as many channels to choose from as we do in today's technologically-driven society, but she was nonetheless living in a manmade version of reality. At the time Esther is introduced on the imperial scene, the king had just finished giving a party. Do you know how long this party lasted? *Six months!* (See Esther 1:3-4.) It doesn't sound like Esther is entering into a place that puts much of a premium on a down-to-earth lifestyle. Nestled safely in the posh, secure lap of the palace, Esther was far from her lonely upbringing without mother or father, far from the dirty slums of Susa, and quite possibly, far from her God.

The question that comes to Esther at this time in her life, in the middle of her dream come true is, "Whose reality are you really living in?" After four glorious years in the luxurious atmosphere of the court, the thought patterns of distraction and denial now must have been status quo. All the blessing and promotion that surrounded Esther's marvelous life story would end up holding her back if she remained unaware of the impending doom set on a collision course for her and her people.

The news of the evil plot against the Jews was not enough, in itself, to shake Esther out of the world she had convinced herself she was living in. Yes she heard the words reported to her, and yes she was "deeply distressed" (Esther 4:4) when she received the news, but her distress did not immediately move her to comparable action. After her initial bout of denial, she sends word to Mordecai, who has just proposed she do something to confront the crisis head-on.

> *Then Esther spoke to Hathach, and gave him a command for Mordecai: "All the king's servants and the people of the king's provinces know that any man or woman who goes into the inner court to the king, who has not been called, he has but one law: put all to death, except the one to whom the king holds out the golden scepter, that he may live. Yet I myself have not been called to go in to the king these thirty days"* (Esther 4:10-11).

In other words, "Mordecai, I realize your situation is bad and I am sorry for it, but you don't understand that if I get involved...if I really get active, it could be inconvenient for me. In fact, my life could be put in danger."

- What did Esther fail to realize?

- What did the Jews in Hitler's Germany fail to realize?

- What did Neville Chamberlain fail to realize?

- What did the Church in Europe in the 1930s fail to realize?

- What are we failing to realize?

Her life, their lives, my life, your life, your children and grandchildren's lives already *are* in danger.

Mordecai's response to Esther revealed to her the truth that brought her to the point of breakthrough at last:

> *Do not think in your heart that you will escape in the king's palace any more than all the other Jews. For if you remain completely silent at this time, relief and deliverance will arise for the Jews from another place,*

but you and your father's house will perish (Esther 4:13-14a).

Unfortunately, sometimes only bad news has the capability of jolting us enough to move us emotionally from where we have been to where we need to be. It is fittingly said that transformation will never happen until the pain of staying as you are becomes greater than the pain of change. Without a doubt, catastrophes have a way of getting us in touch with reality like little else could.

It was a rude awakening for Esther, but an awakening nonetheless. To be jolted out of your reality of choice into a reality in which you have no choice over what happens to you, definitely accounts for a genuine breakthrough. The moment Esther decided to recognize this true reality, she broke through. She realized that as bad as things might get, it would be far worse for her if she did not acknowledge the veracity of Haman's threats.

HISTORY FOR TODAY

As we look back with the hindsight of 20/20 vision, we can see that the choices people made in the face of looming disaster were based on what they, at the end of the day, believed (or told themselves they believed) was really going to happen. Their choices were based on their beliefs, their worldview, their *perceived reality*.

The subject of pre-World War II Germany is both a fascinating and terrifying study. The fact that a civilized nation in the Western world could perpetrate the chilling, efficient mechanisms of death that were achieved by the Third Reich is nothing short of incomprehensible. Entire anthologies, careers, and even institutions of learning have been given to the pursuit of trying to determine what caused otherwise perfectly normal, sane, highly educated and cultured individuals to become one of the most notorious killing regimes in all of history.

In the space of one decade, the nation of Germany went from building a successful Weimar Republic rebounding from the failures of World War I, to systematically massacring one-third of the world's Jewish population. The only thing that is perhaps more mind-boggling than this is how, with few exceptions, no one saw it coming...or cared enough to do anything about it if they did.

By late 1938, German and overall European policy was becoming increasingly anti-Semitic, and things came to a head during what came to be known as *Kristallnacht*—Crystal Night or the Night of the Broken Glass. In October after Poland invalidated the passports of all Polish Jews who had been outside the country for longer than five years, effectively removing their citizenship, Germany jumped on the situation by ordering all such Jews in Germany to leave the country within only two weeks and return to Poland—approximately 17,000 Jews. Those expelled were permitted only one suitcase each and forced to leave by train.

One 17-year-old Jew whose family suffered from the anti-Semitic mandate, took matters into his own hands and shot a German representative at the German embassy in Paris on November 7. After the man died two days later, the Nazis the same evening, November 9, unleashed a massive attack overnight against Jewish synagogues, businesses, and homes, killing a total of 91 Jews and burning nearly 200 synagogues and thousands of shops. This viciously synchronized pogrom throughout Germany and into Austria and Czechoslovakia was an ominous sign that even worse events were in store for future days.[2]

As horrible as Kristallnacht was, many still did not recognize fully what was happening. Did Germany's Jewish population think the worst was over? Did they think this was simply a fluke resurgence of the countless pogroms they had endured throughout European history? To answer our question, we need only to look at the numbers: Thousands of Jews fled Germany after Kristallnacht...but millions chose to stay, in hope that it was a false alarm.

The fact was, most of the world's population didn't want the facts. Those now in influential positions of governance had just come out of what they thought was "the war to end all wars." The truth was, they were about to enter what still to this day qualifies as the most destructive human conflict in recorded history.

Neville Chamberlain was the British Prime Minister who sought to appease Nazi Germany through concessions he made with them in the Munich Agreement. After returning from his conference with Hitler in Munich, he told the citizens of the United Kingdom that there would be "peace for our time." It would be exactly 12 months from the time Neville Chamberlain spoke these infamous words to Hitler's invasion of Poland, which most consider the start of World War II.

Friends, if those in Europe did not awaken to what was really going on until Hitler's threats had become invasions, what will it take to cause us to recognize the reality facing us today?

THE REALITY OF NOW

Consider these examples of what is taking place right now within Western civilization:

In England, where more than 1.8 million Muslims live, prosecutors recently ended four years of inquiry by convicting seven terrorists. One said that Mohammed Hamid (who gave himself the nickname Osama bin London) was candid about his hope that his recruits could dwarf the scale of the 2005 London bombings when 52 people died. Hamid hoped there would be six or seven major attacks before London hosts the 2012 Olympics and talked about killing nonbelievers.[3]

In France, portions of Paris, one of the world's most famous cities, were torched and set in turmoil by radical Muslim youth. Victims included children of African immigrants, and more than 500 vehicles were destroyed in the 2005 deadly and violent upheavals.[4]

In Charlotte, North Carolina, 22-year-old Samir Khan runs an extremist Website from his home in support of al-Qaeda and jihad. As he seeks to rally the radical Muslim faithful, he pronounces: "As for our relation to reviving Jihaad, we turn to the Qur'aan and Sunnah. Allah, the Most High, says, 'Then fight in the Cause of Allah, You are not tasked (held responsible) except for yourself, and incite the believers.' (An-Nisaa: 84)."[5]

From this and many other sources, the call for our own destruction is now emanating from within our own borders. September 11th 2001 was a de facto declaration of war. Like Kristallnacht and like the impending slaughter in ancient Susa, there was time and distance between the declaration and the inevitable outcome; but that was all there was, just time and distance, and each day, every day, there was less time and distance between the Jews and persecution.

> ~ THE CALL FOR OUR DESTRUCTION
> IS EMANATING FROM WITHIN ~
> OUR OWN BORDERS.

Please tell me, if 9/11 was not enough of a wake-up call to mobilize us to focused prayer and determined activism, when will we shake ourselves from our false reality and understand that we are at war?

ARAB AWAKENING

Interestingly enough, there are many from within the greater Arab community who are recognizing that the brand of religion they were born into has anything but humanity's (including their own) best interests in mind.

Several years ago I met Brigitte Gabriel, a Lebanese Christian woman who was born in Marjayoun, Lebanon, and who is the author of *Because They Hate* and the founder of the American Congress for Truth. This courageous woman, not only a

Christian but one from a Muslim culture that is decidedly misogynistic, has become one of the most respected voices speaking out against the dangers of radical Islam today.

Ms. Gabriel grew up in the civil unrest of war-torn Lebanon. Her early years were spent crawling across Muslim sniper lines to help her family survive. It was when she ended up in an Israeli hospital, being compassionately cared for by the very people she had been taught to hate, that her paradigm began to shift. The Israelis' kindness contrasted with the brutality and treachery she experienced at the hands of her own people caused this young mind to reject the anti-Jewish rhetoric rampant in her nation, and to grow in respect and admiration for the Jewish people. Ms. Gabriel has since taken the difficult position of defending Israel in socio-political circles and in global media. Her testimony of personally recognizing reality began when she awakened from a cultural background built on lies. She continues to be a living example of one who has risen from within the Arab community to be a voice for truth.

Nonie Darwish, an active public speaker and writer who was born in Cairo, Egypt, is the author of *Now They Call Me Infidel* and the founder of Arabs for Israel, an organization that promotes support for the state of Israel among Muslim communities throughout the Middle East and beyond. A respected advocate of Arab-Israeli reconciliation, she has worked steadily to raise the level of education in the West regarding the dangers of jihad (Muslim holy war).

Ms. Darwish, like Brigitte Gabriel, was raised in a decidedly anti-Semitic environment. Her father was a commander in the Egyptian Army that brought repeated attacks against the newborn Israeli nation; and he was killed by Israeli forces in 1956 after military advances upon Israel. She has become a prime example of one who has overcome a culture of hate and chosen to identify with God's chosen people despite an opposing influence from within her family. Instead of following in her father's footsteps of being an enemy of Israel, she is now one of Israel's best friends and allies.

The story of Masab Hassan Yousef is uniquely remarkable because of what it has cost him personally to awaken to God's reality. Masab (who now calls himself Joseph) is the son of Sheikh Hassan Yousef, a high-level leader of the Muslim terrorist group Hamas in the West Bank region. Once completely immersed in the radical Muslim lifestyle of terrorism, Masab came to faith in the Jewish Messiah after serving time in prison. He turned his back on Islam, and moved to California where he began a completely new life. Masab said on an interview with Fox News, "I left everything behind me, not only family."

After witnessing Hamas leaders torturing their own comrades during a term of imprisonment they were serving for terrorist activity, he recognized the reality behind the hype of this hate group's anti-Semitic propaganda. Now he boldly declares that there is no chance for Hamas to live peacefully alongside Israel: "Is there any chance for the fire to co-exist with the water? There is no chance."

In knowing the danger to his life in light of the choices he has made, he states with resolve, "They can kill my body but they can't kill my soul."[6]

THREE BATTLEFIELDS

In case it's not apparent to you by now, *we are at war*. I would like to offer some insights into three wars I believe we are fighting—and which I believe Esther fought as well.

1. The Inner War of Self

The first war we must win is the one within ourselves. Our determination to fight the battle within will be what qualifies us for all that is to come. We cannot win any outward battles if we do not first conquer the foes of pride and self-absorption within our own hearts.

Jeremiah 17:9 tells us, "The heart is deceitful above all things, and desperately wicked; who can know it?" We cannot trust our hearts to tell us the truth. We need the Lord to search our hearts and test our minds (see Jer. 17:10) to make sure we are aligned with His thoughts. And how did Esther achieve this proper alignment? She was unchained from self-indulgent philosophies by hearing the voice of the Lord through her covenant relationship with Mordecai.

We need to allow His strength to be our strength in the battle with our own sinful nature, which we must face each day before our feet even touch the floor.

2. The Outer War of Culture

Not only did Esther have to break with a lot of convention to do what she did, she was also acting on behalf of a people who were counter-cultural to prevailing mores. Both of those things will have to be true of us if we are to experience the success she did.

As we consider the anti-Semitism and the anti-Christ spirit that can be found on college campuses, the humanistic philosophies inherent in even that which seems most benign, perhaps we find ourselves thinking, *Things are bad, but they could be worse.* While this is not untrue, I would ask, "What is the determining factor in exactly how bad things are allowed to get?"

If the University of Michigan at Dearborn can allot $25,000 of their state-funded university budget toward accommodating foot baths for Muslim students, I wonder when we are going to get real about what is going on in academia.

The subtle (and not so subtle) infiltration of Islamic fundamentalism into our free society is something that needs to be confronted with equivalent fervor by those who don't want to see exactly how bad things could, in fact, get.

3. The War on Terror

Not only did Esther face a culture war in the palace, she faced the very real threat of the genocide of her people. She faced a virulent anti-Semitism that was determined to wipe out an entire people group from the earth. No doubt about it, Esther found herself in a war against intimidation, cold-blooded murder, and terror.

The war that was declared on terror in 2001 is abating, as the American public's attention and resolve wanes more with each passing day. Europe is now openly referred to as "Eurabia" due to the domination of the Arab/Muslim population infiltrating the borders and political structures of these once-Christian nations. Meanwhile, Mahmoud Ahmadinejad in June 2008 continued to include the United States in his rant against the Jews when he said, "Today, the time for the fall of the satanic power of the United States has come and the countdown to the annihilation of the emperor of power and wealth has started."[7]

Beloved, the enemies of truth, justice, and democratic freedoms are not politically correct, and if we do not recognize their deceptions for what they are, we have no chance of disarming them.

THE REAL JESUS

We have somehow come to embrace a very comfortable and comforting Jesus; the Jesus whose sayings are printed on greetings cards and inspirational bookmarks. But Jesus was anything but a pushover. Ours is a Jesus who overturned tables in His Father's temple and drove out the money-changer with a whip. A Jesus who got in the face of the religious hypocrites of His day and told them what He thought of their shameless duplicity. A Jesus who lovingly, yet firmly, told the adulterous woman who lied about her lover that her story didn't hold weight.

Jesus confronted false realities wherever He found them. He ruthlessly cut to the quick with people because He realized that

121

"tough love" was needed for true change to take place. Jesus was not politically correct in His speech. This was, in one sense, part of what got Him killed. He was in no way out to win a popularity contest, and following the timeline of His ministry reveals that the size of the crowds that followed Him, as well as the number of His disciples, steadily diminished (rather than grew) along the way.

Consider this example from Matthew 16:21-23 of Jesus' interaction with Peter, one of His closest followers and friends:

> From that time Jesus began to show to His disciples that He must go to Jerusalem, and suffer many things from the elders and chief priests and scribes, and be killed, and be raised the third day (Matthew 16:21).

Jesus begins to speak to the reality of the situation—the terror that He, and they, are about to face. He is not mincing words or in any denial. He is plainly warning them to prepare them for what is to come.

> Then Peter took Him aside and began to rebuke Him, saying, "Far be it from You, Lord; this shall not happen to You!" (Matthew 16:22)

Peter obviously cannot handle this information. He turns immediately to denial. He doesn't want any word from the Lord that does not fit with his ideas, his pre-determined optimism.

> But He turned and said to Peter, "Get behind Me, Satan! You are an offense to Me, for you are not mindful of the things of God, but the things of men" (Matthew 16:23).

Ouch. No Jesus meek and mild here, no soothing, sensitive words. Jesus immediately risks offending and losing one of His few remaining supporters by confronting him with cold, hard truth.

Consider a few other promises of Jesus, which have not found their way onto refrigerator magnets:

Then they will deliver you up to tribulation and kill you, and you will be hated by all nations for My name's sake. And then many will be offended, will betray one another, and will hate one another. Then many false prophets will rise up and deceive many. And because lawlessness will abound, the love of many will grow cold. But he who endures to the end shall be saved. And this gospel of the kingdom will be preached in all the world as a witness to all the nations, and then the end will come (Matthew 24:9-14).

Do not think that I came to bring peace on earth. I did not come to bring peace but a sword. For I have come to **"set a man against his father, a daughter against her mother, and a daughter-in-law against her mother-in-law"; and "a man's enemies will be those of his own household."** *He who loves father or mother more than Me is not worthy of Me. And he who loves son or daughter more than Me is not worthy of Me. And he who does not take his cross and follow after Me is not worthy of Me. He who finds his life will lose it, and he who loses his life for My sake will find it* (Matthew 10:34-39).

These and many other Scriptures clearly state that the narrow way of following God in this life will not be easy, and that it will be especially, uniquely perilous for those living in the last days. These words are here so that we can prepare a clear-minded, disciplined, godly approach to the days we are living in. But receiving them requires we leave behind whatever false reality we are living in—even comfortable religious false realities—and embrace the reality that is apparent from both the Word of God and the evening news. These are trying and perilous days for peace-loving people, and especially for those with genuine faith in the God of the Bible.

With all the cultural madness that is swirling around us, what reality are you living in today? *Whose* reality are you recognizing?

In Esther's case, she had to humble herself and admit that she may not have been seeing things through the right lenses, the right perspective. The disciple Peter had to undergo a complete paradigm shift (an inner change) to begin to see things the way Jesus did and become the leader He was asking him to be. Jesus' contemporaries and those from prior times needed to be awakened, and so do we.

It is high time for us to start observing the world around us—really observing. We cannot recognize the reality of today's threat if we don't take the simple step of opening our eyes. We need to become educated about what is taking place in our neighborhoods and our nations.

THE REAL US

Simply put, there is nothing else that more quickly forces us to recognize what we truly believe than being confronted with the worst possible scenario. It is easy to shut the world out by shutting yourself into your own little world—one which you create and control. You can determine what you want to believe and can thereby turn a deaf ear to anything that interferes with your whim and desire. If anything threatens the status quo of your world, you can simply turn up the volume of whatever station you're tuned into until the sirens of warning are deadened by your diversion of choice.

Jamie Buckingham, long-time editor for *Charisma* magazine, used to quote U.S. President James Garfield, who so rightly said, "The truth will set you free, but first it will make you miserable."[8]

May we be those who are unafraid to recognize reality, however wretched we may feel in the process, so that we may become agents of change in the very real and volatile world around us.

No matter what it is you're endeavoring to do, you've got to start somewhere. Recognizing the reality of her situation empowered Esther to begin the process of change. On the heels of what was possibly the most unbearable situation she could have imagined, she found the fortitude, focus, and determination necessary to start taking decisive action. Her first breakthrough opened the door for the quick succession of others that would follow. Now that she had come to terms with reality, she would need to decide what she was going to do to change it.

ENDNOTES

1. http://quotes.maxabout.com/collection/reality/page-0.aspx.

2. Martin Gilbert, *The Jews in the Twentieth Century* (New York: Schocken Books, 2001), 183-184.

3. David Stringer, "Seven Convicted in Terrorist Camps in U.K.," February 2008; http://www.foxnews.com/wires/2008Feb26/0,4670,BritainTerrorTraining,00.html; accessed 6/9/08.

4. "Paris Rioters Set Woman Afire as Violence Spreads"; Associated Press, November 2005; http://www.foxnews.com/story/0,2933,174533,00.html; accessed 6/9/08.

5. http://revolution.muslimpad.com/about-2/;accessed 8/19/08.

6. http://www.foxnews.com/video/?playerId=videolandingpage&referralObject=3018914; accessed 8/21/08.

7. "Ahmadinejad says Israel will soon disappear," Breitbart.com;http://www.breitbart.com/article.php?id=080602124328.f6eyi8y1&show_article=1; accessed 6/6/08.

8. James A. Garfield, quoted at http://thinkexist.com/quotation/the_truth_will_set_you_free-but_first_it_will/212794.html; accessed 8/30/08.

CHAPTER 8

~

BREAKTHROUGH #2—CRYING OUT

There is a mighty lot of difference
between saying prayers and praying.[1]
—John G. Lake

More things are wrought by prayer
than this world dreams of.[2]
—Alfred Lord Tennyson

Mordecai's cry came at a critical moment in Esther's life, a time when she needed to be awakened from her false reality to the true, dangerous reality of her situation. The power of Mordecai's words served as the catalyst she needed to shed the self-induced shell of distraction and denial. It took something to wake her up to the dire straits she found herself in, and if the king's edict did not, the power of a trusted spiritual father (indeed, even a surrogate natural father) speaking into her life did just that.

But now she would face yet another decisive moment. It was not enough that Esther awakened to the reality of her situation. *Now she must act!* The very first action someone takes under such conditions reveals everything to us about their character and belief system. What would Esther's first reaction be? What is the first step she will take now that she realizes she is in a serious predicament? A thousand concerns vied for Esther's attention simultaneously.

What could she possibly say to the king that would avert his certain anger at her approaching him without being summoned?

What about her reputation and fate, which could very soon resemble that of the disgraced Queen Vashti?

If the worst were to happen, where would she go and how would she survive?

What about the safety of her beloved Uncle Mordecai, and, for that matter, her extended Jewish family?

What would her first step be? Now that she was awakened and active, how would she order her priorities?

The story is no different for us when we are faced with harsh circumstances, unforeseen challenges, or battles that emerge in our lives. In a moment of panic, everything calls out to us to act first and pray later. But in the midst of the deluge of fear and anxiety Esther miraculously and gloriously remembered to put first things first. She remembered to do what was most needed—beseech the power of Heaven.

> ~ IN A MOMENT OF PANIC EVERY-
> THING CALLS OUT TO US TO ACT ~
> FIRST AND PRAY LATER.

Esther did not check the treasury, consult with military advisors, or seek the wisdom of court insiders. She did not, primarily, rely on her own strength, or even the strength of others. She understood that none of these things could ultimately bring the answer she needed. She was about to engage in a spiritual encounter that required she possess heavenly authority. Esther's primary response was not relying on her own thoughts or imaginations; her first response was to *cry out* to the Lord.

> *"Go, gather all the Jews who are present in Shushan, and fast for me; neither eat nor drink for three days, night or day. My maids and I will fast likewise. And so I will go to the king, which is against the law; and if I perish, I perish!" So Mordecai went his way and did according to all that Esther commanded him* (Esther 4:16-17).

Whatever the condition of her heart had been before the crisis, Esther now realized that her situation demanded a reaction that would access the portals of Heaven and bring answers down for the rapidly deteriorating condition of her people's welfare. Esther needed the favor of King Ahasuerus and she needed it quickly, but Esther was wise enough to understand that the only way to obtain favor from her king was to first obtain the favor of the King of kings, who had preserved her people through the Red Sea, the wilderness of Sinai, and the burning of Jerusalem at the hand of the Babylonians.

THE HUMILITY OF PRAYER

Scripture is full of hundreds of stories with one essential lesson: You can't do this on your own. You really do need God.

In story after story, we watch people decide if they are going to have the humility to walk things out God's way or try it on their own. And time after time we see that the "arm of flesh" (humankind's natural wisdom) fails, and that Heaven's wisdom (though oftentimes foolish in the eyes of the world) always triumphs.

We are left with the proven truth: earthly battles really do require heavenly victories. When enemies surround the people of God, it is then that the people must humbly join together with a united voice and ask for heaven's intervention. This is the theme of the corporate cry of God's people in Psalm 20:

Now I know that the Lord saves His anointed; **He will answer him from His holy heaven with the saving strength of His right hand.** *Some trust in chariots, and some in horses; but we will remember the name of the Lord our God. They have bowed down and fallen; but we have risen and stand upright. Save, Lord! May the King answer us when we call* (Psalm 20:6-9).

If tough times expose what is within us, then the story of Esther reveals that she was a woman of genuine humility, seeking God's help from the place of desperation. Though she could have persisted in the pitfalls of distraction and denial, she understood that, queen though she was, she did not possess within herself the power to save a nation. She needed help, and she knew it. Having been awakened from what had temporarily paralyzed her, her new and true reality moved her to do what was actually needed.

Esther had tapped into the power of what Matthew 5:3 says: "Blessed are the poor in spirit, for theirs is the kingdom of heaven."

In other words...

Blessed are the humble of heart, who are in touch with their own complete helplessness, and who know that they must turn to Him who is "a very present help in trouble" (Ps. 46:1).

Blessed are the broken, who are not too proud to admit that in their flesh dwells "no good thing" (Rom. 7:18 KJV).

Blessed are the desperate, who realize there is only one way out of their situation—the one disclosed by God in the place of prayer.

In this vein, Esther cast off the outer covering of her royal robes and cried out with all her might—not only in word but in deed as well. With the enemy at her doorstep, Esther laid hold of another powerful spiritual key that is vital for us individually in our spiritual battles, and absolutely necessary if the

Church, as a corporate Esther, is to stand against the Hamans who are rising around the world, threatening once again. Esther called a city-wide fast.

Prayer is powerful, and prayer with fasting is *seriously* powerful. Fasting is prayer on steroids.

∼ FASTING IS PRAYER ON STEROIDS. ∼

Esther understood, as we are coming to understand, that there are battles that can only be won through corporate, desperate, persevering, LOUD, travailing prayer and fasting.

When Esther all of a sudden realized that it was *not* all about her, her feasting turned to fasting, and she gained authority in another realm.

As the Hebrews under King Jehoshaphat faced the daunting multitude of Moabites and Ammonites encroaching upon Judah, their response was to gather together from all the cities in Judah to seek the Lord. As they prayed and prophesied in the presence of the Lord, the word came to them that they did not need to fear, but only stand firm and see the salvation of the Lord. When they went out the next morning to meet their enemies, they found them destroying one another! (See Second Chronicles 20.) Because the nation had prioritized prayer and fasting, the Lord had given them a victory infinitely more astounding than if they had warred in their own human strength.

Like Jehoshaphat in Judah, Esther's decision brought into an extremely volatile situation the transformational power of corporate fasting.

What was needed in Esther's day was a corporate victory on par with, perhaps even greater than, those won by Gideon, Joshua, David, and Jehoshaphat; and she knew that in order to get breakthrough, she would need to enlist the help of every living, breathing member of their extended community. As it has always been, Esther knew that only collective faith brings corporate conquest.

A Spiritual Battle for a Spiritual Victory

I believe the greatest battle Esther faced in this situation was the war that raged within her—a spiritual battle in which heavenly and demonic forces were actively involved. She had to make a decision to humble herself, and it took every ounce of spiritual strength she had to be faithful in the midst of this struggle.

The forces of darkness do not want us to humble ourselves because the enemy knows the power of a life submitted, a life ready to carry out the commands of Scripture and the Word of the Lord. The enemy will rage against you if you truly decide to believe in the power of God. The enemy will try to keep you from accessing that authority by employing the practical measures and heart posture of humility.

Aside from Esther's personal spiritual battle at this critical moment, this also was a very real battle for the future of God's chosen people. The testimony of God's covenant with His own people was at stake. The forces of darkness brought an all-out assault against the Jewish nation, spouting forth from evil Haman, and sought to keep Esther and anyone else from stopping it. By deciding to take action, she was stepping out into the heat of a battle that was much bigger than her own life. She had been positioned by God for this critical moment, and both Heaven and hell were watching to see what her response would be.

It would be a gross underestimation to view the circumstances of Esther's day as a battle against a single evil man named Haman (though evil always has a door of entry). Esther's battle was a battle that was generations old—a quest to wipe out the testimony of God's faithfulness in the earth—a battle that still rages today.

Scripture tells us that our "adversary the devil walks about like a roaring lion, seeking whom he may devour" (1 Pet. 5:8). To fight spiritual battles, we, like Esther, must fight with spiritual weapons. Spiritual battles simply cannot be won solely on the strength of man and his strategies. Divine intervention is needed, and only the humble will recognize this truth.

A CULTURE OF PRAYER

Deuteronomy 6 gives us a picture of the strength of the Jewish community throughout the ages—the history of a people who have been committed to a lifestyle of prayer in the glories of Solomon's Temple and in the horrors of Hitler's Auschwitz.

For centuries the one watchword above all, the *cry* of a people, has been, "Hear, O Israel: The Lord our God, the Lord is One!" (Deut. 6:4). For the Jews, prayer has always been just as much a cry to man as it was a cry to God; at once a word of exhortation to the community, and a plea to the Almighty. To cry out to God *is* to cry out to our neighbors and to pray for others. Without stirring up the people to action, there cannot be a victory over the greatest enemy of all—prayerlessness.

~ THE GREATEST ENEMY OF ALL—PRAYERLESSNESS. ~

The Hebrew families, according to God's command, instructed their children at morning, noon, and night to engage in a lifestyle of prayer within their covenant community. When sitting up, when lying down, when going out, and when coming in, the Jewish people *pray*. If they laid hold of this reality and lived their daily lives centered on this truth, they were unstoppable and all the nations around lived in fear of them. If they forsook this calling and sought to follow their own ways, they fell into the hands of their enemies until they again sought the face of God.

To be an observant Jew is to be a person of prayer. The Israelite nation of Esther's day had previously fallen into the hands of the Babylonians, who were then conquered by the Persians led by Cyrus the Great. When Esther sent the notice throughout the Persian kingdom to join as one in prayer and fasting, though the people were living in a foreign land as a result of their prior disobedience, she hoped they would respond. She hoped that because of their shared history and culture of prayer, they would understand the importance of the call and mobilize into the prayer army they were created to be.

MAKING A MARK ON HISTORY

The inspiration and example of the Jewish people as a community of prayer has resulted in the raising up of other communities of prayer throughout Church history. These communities, strengthened by the heritage of God's dealings with His people throughout salvation history, would never have existed had it not been for the reality of the covenant people of God who obeyed His command to live lives of prayer. Through the strength afforded by God, these communities have carried the torch—the flame—of God's presence, which can only be tended through corporate, committed prayer.

One such landmark community was the Moravians of Herrnhut, Germany, who were best known for two things: effective prayer and far-reaching missions. To say that these two aspects of the Moravian legacy were tied together is an understatement. The fuel for their lasting legacy was the ongoing flame of corporate prayer, which sent them forth into the nations of the world to spread the power of the Gospel.

Count Nikolaus Ludwig von Zinzendorf, the founder of Herrnhut and leader of the movement that eventually became known as the Moravian Church, was not a typical aristocrat in 18th-century Europe. He opened his personal estate to persecuted Christian believers from many walks of life—a somewhat strange assortment of devoted Pietists who were largely outcasts from the state churches.

Under Zinzendorf's leadership, the believers at Herrnhut, (which means "the Lord's watch") enacted an astounding historical accomplishment: a documented period (beginning in 1727) of 100 consecutive years of organized, uninterrupted night and day prayer. This level of commitment to a lifestyle of prayer and a structure of covenantal community paid enormous dividends in the lives of the Moravians.

Later in Esther's story, the message of her people's victory through crying out in prayer and fasting was sent forth into all the provinces in the Persian kingdom in their various languages and cultures. Similarly, the Moravians went forth to the nations of the earth from the place of active prayer, carrying to many languages and cultures the Eternal King's victorious decree that salvation and redemption had been made accessible through Jesus Christ. Their avid commitment to the Kingdom of God translated into social action and unique strategies for advancing the Kingdom throughout the earth. These zealous men and women even went so far as to sell themselves into slavery so that they could reach the growing population of exploited peoples in the New World.[3]

Because the Moravians intentionally gave themselves to a lifestyle of intercession, the fruit of their lives is still evident in today's world. They are among those in history's pages who, like Esther, cried out and subsequently changed the world. Their unfailing, ardent prayers moved them to uncompromising, passionate action. Today, nearly 300 years later, the legacy of the Moravians lives on because this imperfect yet persevering community of believers lived out what they prayed, from the place of crying out to the Lord.

In our day, God desires to raise us up again to become a courageous people like Esther, the Moravians, and many others who are committed to the call of corporate prayer and fasting.

Prayer meetings are not only for 12 precious older ladies who gather together on Tuesday nights in some back room of the church. (Though thank God for them—who knows where we would be without them!) No, prayer is for the entire house of God—day and night and night and day—to rise up and cry out to the Lord as a nation of priests!

The time has come for the men of God to take their place as chief priests and intercessors for their homes, to bless their children, to command blessing over their communities, cities, and nations.

Where are the wailing women who will cry out over a world lost in the depravity of sin, who will travail and birth forth the purposes of God for their children and their grandchildren?

We must release the little ones to cry out "Hosanna" in the Temple, declaring the Lordship of the man Jesus Christ (see Matt. 21:15), and apply the purity of their faith to a world more in need of His miracles than ever.

People of God, it is time for us to *pray*! Is anyone hearing the proclamation of the prophet Joel for our day?

> *Blow the trumpet in Zion, consecrate a fast, call a sacred assembly; gather the people, sanctify the congregation, assemble the elders, gather the children and nursing babes; let the bridegroom go out from his chamber, and the bride from her dressing room. Let the priests, who minister to the Lord, weep between the porch and the altar; let them say, "Spare Your people, O Lord"* (Joel 2:15-17a).

If we recognize the reality of the threat facing Israel and the Church (and all of Western civilization) today, will we shake our heads and say, "What a shame about what's happening to the world..." or will we rise up and do the only thing we can do: call for divine help?

MODERN MOVEMENTS

A dedicated few have established prayer and fasting movements today that have helped to reignite the flame of the presence of the Lord as in years past. Events like the National Day of Prayer[4] and the Global Day of Prayer[5] have reached every part of our nation and beyond, and have focused us again on the centrality of prayer during the time in which we live.

The International House of Prayer in Kansas City[6] has mobilized an army of worshiping intercessors crying out to the Lord day and night continually (24/7/365) since September 19, 1999, igniting an international movement that has summoned believers everywhere to active participation in Houses of Prayer around the world. TheCall, which is a movement of Christians to plant "prayer furnaces" throughout the United States to fast and pray for revival, has brought together generations of believers who are desperate for revival and real change in our nation.

Those who have led such movements know that there are windows in history that open and allow for a change in the atmosphere. Great revolutions occur (for good or evil) in the vacuum created by these openings. It is in these seasons that key men and women—sometimes entire generations—risk everything to ensure that what needs to go, goes; and what needs to come, comes.

According to TheCall director Lou Engle, "When there is no hope, when there is no remedy, God still has a holy prescription."[7] This is the essence of "crying out." More than an event, TheCall (and movements like it) represent a fast, not a festival—a call for societal reformation.

In the book *The Call of the Elijah Revolution*, Lou Engle and James W. Goll ask:

> What would happen if tens of thousands or hundreds of thousands of spiritual fathers and mothers committed themselves to prayer and fasting for the breaking of the

spirit of Jezebel over their lives and the lives of their children? ...What would happen if they interceded for their children that a "double portion" spirit would be poured out on their "Elishas" and "Jehus"? What would happen? Nothing short of a revolution! ...It is time for the Body of Christ to return to committed, radical, righteous living in a day of moral decadence. It's time for passion and sacrifice to call forth radical change.[8]

One of the most remarkable prayer developments of our time has been the grassroots movement of the Day of Prayer for the Peace of Jerusalem (DPPJ)[9] spearheaded by Eagles' Wings Ministries, which on the first Sunday of every October has mobilized more than 170 nations around the world to pray in accordance with the Scriptural mandate from Psalm 122:6-8:

> *Pray for the peace of Jerusalem: "May they prosper who love you. Peace be within your walls, prosperity within your palaces." For the sake of my brethren and my companions, I will now say, "Peace be within you."*

In this, the single largest Jerusalem-focused prayer initiative in the history of the Church, the DPPJ has awakened millions of believers around the globe to honor our Jewish heritage by standing in the gap for Israel, the root that supports those of us who have been grafted in (see Rom. 11:18).

If there is one motivation I feel is lacking in the Body of Christ, it is the centrality and importance of standing faithfully with natural Israel in our prayers. This is the secret key ingredient for us to become furnaces of effective, breakthrough prayer all around the globe. Only as we align our values and our prayers with the covenants that God has established with the Jewish people, will our prayers be effective in the greatest and most powerful ways, as God intended them to be.

Dr. Jack Hayford, who co-chairs the DPPJ along with me, says of the importance of praying for Israel, "There is no more critical issue today to help us align our prayers with God's

Kingdom and God's heart than the issue of standing with Israel and praying for the peace of Jerusalem. The purposes of God are advanced mightily when we stand first with His covenant land and people."

If we are to unite and forcefully advance the Kingdom of God in our generation, we must take our place as "watchmen on the walls" of Jerusalem and declare that we will "not keep silent, and give Him no rest till He establishes and till He makes Jerusalem a praise in the earth" (Isa. 62:6-7).

On May 15, 2008, in conjunction with the celebration of the 60th anniversary of the founding of the modern state of Israel, Eagles' Wings held the 4th Annual Jerusalem Prayer Banquet at the United Nations in New York City. More than 500 guests filled the dining room for this historic evening that was the first-ever Jerusalem prayer event of its kind at the UN, including the attendance of hundreds of Jewish and Christian spiritual, business, and political leaders.

The Jerusalem Prayer Banquet, which was recorded and rebroadcast by GOD TV, concluded with a time of prayer with both Christian leaders and Jewish leaders praying blessings over Israel. Many of the guests said they had never been part of such a powerful evening. Some of the Jewish guests remarked on the significance of the evening, saying it was a night they would never forget. This message must become a formative wake-up call for our time—the determination to pray effectively, often, and fervently for the furthering of the Kingdom of God in Israel and the nations.

It is incumbent upon us to cry out to the Lord—especially in these days when it is so obvious that the house of Islam is increasingly filling with radicals bent on the destruction of all they call "infidels" (non-Muslims). Christian men in particular need to stand up and bravely face the future. The mosques are full of men willing to stand up for what they believe—our men must stand firm if we are to contend for a world allowing people the freedom to worship according to the dictates of their own conscience.

Secularism is against prayer altogether. It forbids prayer in school. It forbids it in the courts—not even allowing the display of the Ten Commandments, from which our judicial system derives its core morality. But we are called to impact every realm of our society with the power of prayer.

A CALLING TO CRY OUT

I am convinced that the corporate Church in the United States doesn't believe in prayer. I just don't think we believe in it. I cannot think of any other reason why we wouldn't do it. We don't pray long and hard in our comfortable, Western churches—not like they do in Nigeria or South Korea or Brazil—at least not yet, as persecution has not yet begun in earnest. But I believe that God is doing a work in raising up a house to contend with other houses of prayer in the earth. I believe He is raising up *His* house of prayer.

> *My* house shall be called a house of prayer for all nations (Isaiah 56:7).

In this critical moment of human history, it is not enough for us, as a modern-day corporate Esther, to merely perceive the reality of what is happening on our watch. We must become like the sons of Issachar, who understood the times *and knew what to do* (see 1 Chron. 12:32). And the very first thing we must do is *cry out*. Living lifestyles of fervent, sustained, desperate intercession is the only way we will know how to navigate through the difficult days ahead. We must corporately lay hold of Heaven for supernatural help and supernatural strategies—and we must do it right now.

~ WE MUST CORPORATELY LAY
HOLD OF HEAVEN FOR ~

SUPERNATURAL HELP AND SUPERNATURAL STRATEGIES—AND WE MUST DO IT RIGHT NOW.

Let us therefore come boldly to the throne of grace, that we may obtain mercy and find grace to help in time of need (Hebrews 4:16).

Esther's example speaks to us today. When it seems all hope is lost, when it seems you don't know what to do, and when you're tempted to take matters into your own hands, lift your hands to Heaven.

- Pray.
- Fast.
- Because there is a God in Heaven who hears and answers.

ENDNOTES

1. http://www.tentmaker.org/Quotes/prayer quotes.htm.

2. http://thinkexist.com/quotations/prayer/4.html.

3. http://www.moravian.org/history/; accessed 8/29/08.

4. www.ndptf.org.

5. www.globaldayofprayer.com.

6. www.ihop.org.

7. http://www.thecall.com.

8. Lou Engle and James Goll, *The Call of the Elijah Revolution* (Shippensburg, PA: Destiny Image Publishers, 2008), 137-138.

9. www.daytopray.com.

CHAPTER 9

~

BREAKTHROUGH #3— DETERMINED CONVICTIONS

The hottest places in hell are reserved for those who, in a time of moral crisis, maintain their neutrality.[1]
—Dante, The Inferno

Living by our convictions is not something we tend to hear a lot about these days. From multi-millionaire CEOs wreaking havoc in the markets and the lives of thousands through fraudulent business transactions, to scandals within the Church, everywhere it seems the ethical standards that were once the bedrock of society are now considered, at the very least, outdated. Moral conviction is something to be questioned, suspicious of, and challenged, rather than celebrated. Tolerance is the new virtue, and it trumps moral conviction.

The more I study conflicts throughout human history, the more intrigued I become by the choices people make and why. I find myself asking the question, *What makes someone either a coward or a hero?*

In any conflict, there are always three parties: the perpetrators, the victims, and the bystanders. What distinguishes these three groups is the level of choice they possess within the situation.

- The perpetrators are those whose choice is in operation, whose choice has even created the conflict.

- The victims are those with limited choice—who are suffering at the hands of others' choices and must struggle to see even the slightest sign of hope for change in their situations.

- Unlike the perpetrators, the bystanders don't come into the situation already having chosen; but unlike the victims, they have the power to make their own choice. The bystanders have to choose which side of the conflict they're going to identify with.[2]

So what is it that leads one bystander to make the right (heroic) choice, and what causes another to make the wrong (cowardly) choice?

Our courage (which we will look into more in the next chapter) always comes from our convictions, those beliefs we hold at the core of our being. I believe that, by and large, those who display admirable outer convictions are those who have not silenced the inner voice of conviction within themselves, and are living before God with a clear conscience. They live in the righteous fear of God, and so are not afraid of man.

THOSE WHO DISPLAY ADMIRABLE OUTER CONVICTIONS ARE THOSE WHO HAVE NOT SILENCED THE INNER VOICE OF CONVICTION.

Mordecai was a man of deep conviction. Remember, this is actually what got him into trouble with Haman in the first place. You'll recall how Mordecai's refusal to kowtow to Haman's pride marked him as unique—as a man who wouldn't give one inch to unrighteousness.

Can't you just see him now as he walked to his position at the palace gate each morning, resolutely maintaining his dignity as he passed Haman by? It's not that Mordecai wanted Haman to hate him, but people who have no integrity naturally resent anyone who does.

ROYAL CONVICTIONS

Scene: 20th-century Denmark, as Hitler's soon-to-be global conflict begins to unfurl across Europe. Here we meet King Christian X of Denmark. Seen as an archaic figurehead, the aging monarch did not appear to be destined for popularity among his subjects. The fact that he was able to spawn the most effective state resistance movement against the Nazis is what makes this account of personal conviction as impressive as it is inspiring.

When the Nazis invaded the nations of Europe, many European monarchs vacated their thrones and fled to Great Britain. But Christian X remained where his sense of duty had always held him—with his people. Throughout the years of the occupation, the elderly king continued to make his daily horseback ride, unarmed and unguarded, down the streets of Copenhagen. It is not difficult to imagine him as he must have been: dignified, proper, and in no way given to acquiesce in any matter he deemed ethically questionable.

His simple display of self-assurance, of consistent presence, communicated, if ever so quietly, a marked defiance toward the gun-clad troops that had stationed themselves within his kingdom. It must also have made an impression on the citizens of Denmark who responded to the trespassers with similar insubordination.

Although initially accommodating to the occupying German army, the Danish citizens grew increasingly resentful of them. Several years after the initial invasion, the Danes began to wear visible tokens of their opposition: square pins displaying their national flag and the king's emblem fastened to their shirts as a show of national solidarity.

In addition to voicing his opposition toward the Nazis in his speeches, there are reports of Christian X snubbing Hitler, as he did upon receiving a flattering birthday greeting from the evil dictator. In reply, the noble king sent what was the most extravagant show of appreciation his conscience would allow, "My best thanks."[3] At this, the outraged Hitler cut all ambassadorial relations between the two countries, and rescinded his now-defunct well-wishes.

As the years progressed, so did Hitler's plot to deal with the alleged "problem" of international Jewry. As the Nazis marched toward their Final Solution, they planned an invasion of Denmark in which they would gather all the Jews living within her borders and deport them to concentration camps.

Word leaked that Nazi forces were going to carry out this mission on October 1, coincidentally the Jewish New Year in 1943. The citizens of Denmark responded with immediate and decisive action. They took their Jewish neighbors into their homes to hide them until they could be shuttled to safety in nearby Sweden. The Danish police force and coast guard refused to cooperate with the Nazis in their search efforts. Many German soldiers on the ground were persuaded to turn a blind eye. The people of Denmark united to orchestrate this impromptu rescue operation, and, in a matter of days, delivered nearly the entirety of Denmark's Jewish population to safety on foreign shores using the one means of transportation available to them: fishing boats.

The few hundred who were not rescued, but captured and interned at a work camp, were assiduously cared for by their fellow countrymen and kept alive despite their dismal living conditions. Through diplomatic persuasion, Danish leaders implored the Nazis not to send their Jewish nationals to the death camps, and, incredibly, their appeal was granted. Most of these Jewish victims survived to see V-E Day (Victory in Europe Day, May 8, 1945).

As if that weren't amazing enough, when the displaced Jews returned to their homes, they found them not pillaged and seized by the Gentile citizenry (as in most other places in Europe where the Jews' personal property was up for grabs), but rather kept in good condition for them by their neighbors.

The people of Denmark united to execute a successful civilian rescue operation that saved virtually its entire Jewish population from extinction at the hands of the Nazis' Final Solution.

This astounding account of resistance at a national level has created a standard of conduct we have the moral obligation to emulate. In this one nation, the Nazis' efforts toward systematic annihilation were averted, thanks to the bold and selfless actions of the Danish people. And to think, it all began with an elderly king who refused to let the bully kick him off of his throne.

Thrilling, isn't it? It's always awe-inspiring to hear stories like this. But I always end up wondering, *If that were me, if I had been in his shoes, would I have acted as resolutely as he?* And what about you? If your life decisions (not what you *said*, but just what you *did*) were recorded in the annals of human history, what would your life *say* about you?

IF YOUR LIFE DECISIONS WERE RECORDED, WHAT WOULD YOUR LIFE *SAY* ABOUT YOU?

Mordecai's convictions, like many others' throughout time, have left a clear testimony of what it means when someone stands firm on principle. Whether standing against what was wrong, or for what was right, Mordecai was a person of deep conviction. But it was not Mordecai in the palace. It was not Mordecai in the position to appeal to the king. It was Esther. Was Esther a person of determined conviction? She probably admired Mordecai's convictions, but did she have any of her own?

As we have seen from the first half of her story, Esther was a very passive character. She was raised to know right from wrong; but, at the end of the day, who was she really? We know who Mordecai was—his actions made that clear from the start. But when the ball is passed to Esther, we're suddenly wondering what choice she will make. In a moment, in an instant, it all comes down to what *she* believes. Did Esther know her convictions? Do we know ours?

Just a few chapters ago, you read about Esther's inner transformation and studied her famous line, "I will go to the king even though it is against the law, and if I perish, I perish!" Esther was faced with a choice when she came to her even-though moment. Would she abide by the law and not jeopardize her relationship with the king? Or would she shed her docile image and lay down her own reputation for the sake of her people?

~ OUR CONVICTIONS, AT THE END OF THE DAY, ARE WHAT WE ARE WILLING TO *DO* ABOUT WHAT WE BELIEVE. ~

After recognizing the reality of her situation and crying out to God for mercy, and before making her decision to go before the king, Esther had to determine her convictions. Our convictions determine our actions, and our actions, in turn, determine our destiny. Our convictions are not what we would like to think we believe or what we admire about what others believe. Our convictions, at the end of the day, are what we are willing to **do** about what we believe. This is who we truly are.

EVEN-THOUGH MOMENTS

*Go, gather together all the Jews who are in Susa, and fast for me. Do not eat or drink for three days, night or day. I and my maids will fast as you do. When this is done, I will go to the king, **even though** it is against the law. And if I perish, I perish* (Esther 4:16 NIV).

Not all even-though moments are as dramatic as Esther's. People make seemingly insignificant choices every day that actually determine more of our individual and collective futures than we might be able to imagine. From presidents in the board room to parents in the dining room to students in the classroom, we all face an even-though moment—a time when we must take a stand—no matter what the consequences.

No doubt you can recall even-though moments in your own life. Maybe it was the time you raised the standard of righteousness in your workplace even though you knew your boss wouldn't like it. Maybe it was the time you voiced disagreement over a professor's biased remark even though you knew it could result in a lower grade. Or the time you took an unpopular stand at the PTA meeting. Maybe it was the time you chose to go home after work even though the "big players" were going out for happy hour.

I am convinced that God is bringing every believer to an even-though moment. He is bringing us to a place where we become aware of the price to be paid; of the fact that there are certain choices we've been given to make, the outcome of which extend far beyond our current scope of understanding.

Scripture provides no shortage of examples for us to follow in our desire to walk out our faith in real and uncompromising ways:

The three Hebrew lads, Shadrach, Meshach, and Abed-Nego were, like Esther, living in exile and under the patronage of a pagan king. When faced with his ultimatum of bowing down before the colossal idol he had erected, they encountered their even-though moment. They could choose to worship the false god, or be thrown into a fiery furnace.

If we're honest, we would have at least been tempted to do a small, polite bow to the statue to save our skin. After all, what would be the harm in that? Isn't it man who looks at the outward image, and God who looks at the heart? They could have rationalized their way out of this situation any number of ways, and what really would have been the problem with that?

∽ THE ONLY THING COMPROMISE ∽ ACTUALLY SUCCEEDS IN DOING IS PROLONGING THE INEVITABLE.

What we need to keep in mind is that the only thing compromise actually succeeds in doing is prolonging the inevitable. Eventually, those we have sought to placate will fulfill their avowed aggression toward us. As Winston Churchill so aptly put it, "An appeaser is one who feeds a crocodile, hoping it will eat him last."[4]

These three young men knew that straddling the fence doesn't count, and their audacious answer to the king's demand boasts every bit as much courage as did Esther's. Look at their even-though moment:

> O Nebuchadnezzar, we do not need to defend ourselves before you in this matter. If we are thrown into the blazing furnace, the God we serve is able to save us from it, and he will rescue us from your hand, O king. But **even if he does not**, we want you to know, O king, that we will not serve your gods or worship the image of gold you have set up (Daniel 3:16b-18 NIV).

These are not alone in their legacy of faith. Abraham raised a knife to sacrifice Isaac *even though* he was his only son. Moses went to Pharaoh on behalf of his people *even though* he didn't think he was the right man for the job. Solomon asked for wisdom *even though* he could have asked for money and merriment. Mary said yes to the angel's annunciation of her pregnancy *even though* she was unwed. Jesus died on the cross *even though* He could have lived forever as the incorruptible Man on earth.

Where would we be right now if any of these had decided to go in a different direction? And do we realize that future generations will look back and ask the same question of us?

OUR CHOICE

No one can make our choices for us. It is not enough to simply attend all the right services, read all the right Scriptures, relate to all the right people, and say all the right things. It will always be what we, in our heart of hearts, are convicted of that we resort to when push comes to shove.

God honored all those in the Bible with determined convictions, many with deliverance in this world, others with the glory of martyrdom and achieving an eternal inheritance in the next. Daniel wasn't lunch for the lions. The trio didn't become torches in the furnace. Esther's king didn't behead her. David's Goliath didn't trample him under his big boot. God became their defense, their high tower of strength. And now we have the opportunity of allowing God to be faithful to us in our even-though moments of valiant decision.

There's a short verse in the Book of Esther that is easy to miss, but that has always, for some reason, caught my attention. It is the very next verse after Esther's, "if I perish, I perish." Listen to this intriguing turn of events, which immediately follows Esther's declaration and instruction that a fast be called in Susa: "So Mordecai went away and did just as Esther had commanded him" (Esther 4:17 NASB).

151

Wasn't it always the other way around? Esther listening to her caretaker's prudent and seasoned counsel? All of a sudden, Mordecai is taking orders from the inexperienced young woman! Once we know our convictions, everything changes, including our own selves.

~ ONCE WE KNOW OUR CONVIC-TIONS, EVERYTHING CHANGES. ~

I believe this is an illustration of how the Holy Spirit desires not only to speak *to* us, but also to speak *through* us. I'm sure Mordecai was thrilled to see Esther finally stepping into her true identity and now beseeching *him* to act on *her* behalf. What an amazing portrait of the intercessory power of the Holy Spirit! "The Spirit Himself *intercedes for us* with groanings too deep for words," (Rom. 8:26 NASB). God actually desires to partner with us in the mission we're given to accomplish. The Gospel of Mark states that after Jesus ascended, the disciples went out to fulfill The Great Commission, "the Lord working *with* them" (Mark 16:20). How humbling! This partnering with us is a way in which God honors those who have determined to honor Him.

This is not to say that sticking to your convictions does not come at a price. Saints of old, as well as those today, have paid a very high price, and have often paid the ultimate price, to do just that.

I'm reminded of Casper ten Boom, an elderly Dutchman who held a staunch belief that the Jews were God's chosen people. Casper owned a watch shop and home in Haarlem where his daughter Corrie and other children grew up. A conservative family from the Dutch Reformed Church, the ten Booms taught their children to love the Jewish people and to serve God and others. Although his wife Cor died in 1921, Casper continued to model a godly lifestyle for his children throughout his later years when World War II broke out and the Germans invaded the Netherlands in 1940.

Casper knew what he was living for, and after his own children were grown and some moved out, he took in 11 more homeless children and raised them as his own.[5] It was his convictions during war-time (a legacy which he passed on to his family) that have inspired countless numbers of believers to identify themselves with the seed of Abraham even during times of persecution. Determined to do what was right in God's eyes, the ten Booms provided a safe haven for many Jews behind a false wall in Corrie's bedroom, as documented in the remarkable book, *The Hiding Place,* by Corrie ten Boom.

Casper's strong convictions are exemplified by an instance in which a Jewish mother and prematurely-born infant were brought to his door, seeking safety. Corrie had been asking a pastor who was visiting their watch shop if he would take the child into his home outside the city where the rogue authorities would be less likely to discover him. When the pastor exclaimed he could lose his life if he took the child in, Casper swept up the child in his arms and responded, "You say we could lose our lives for this child. I would consider that the greatest honor that could come to my family."[6]

Not many years later, after having been arrested by the police under suspicion of harboring Jews, Casper, who was 84 years of age at the time, was offered the chance to return to his home in peace because of his old age. The interrogators' one condition was that he pledge to cease his illegal activity of sheltering Jews. Casper's instantaneous and honest reply was, "If I go home today, tomorrow I will open my door again to any man in need who knocks." Casper was then taken into Nazi custody—dying just days later—because he had determined his convictions and stuck by them to the end.

WORTH FIGHTING FOR

As I pointed out at the start of this chapter, people who don't have sound moral convictions are always at odds with those who do. This often creates tension between the parties.

It's not that people of conviction want war, it's just that they refuse to substitute false peace for true.

Jesus says in the Beatitudes, "Blessed are the peacemakers, for they shall be called sons of God" (Matt. 5:9), which I believe is often mistaken for a call to acquiesce to dissidents. But the text is very clear when it says, "peace*makers*." Sometimes it takes making war to make peace. United States President Franklin Delano Roosevelt put it so aptly when he pronounced, "If I must choose between righteousness and peace, I choose righteousness."[7]

War is a terrible thing, and we as servants of God have the obligation to work for, long for, and pray for peace. Sometimes, though, we have the duty to fight for peace as well. History reveals the errancy of ignoring, due to our own moral cowardice, the indefensible actions of those who hate peace.

~ HISTORY REVEALS THE ERRANCY OF IGNORING THE INDEFENSIBLE ACTIONS OF THOSE WHO HATE PEACE. ~

David was a man of war. Even his youth was spent slaying bears and giants. We remember the daughters of Israel singing out, "Saul has slain his thousands, and David his tens of thousands" (1 Sam. 18:7 NIV). Interestingly, it is during a time when David is not on the battlefield with his men that we find him ensnared in an abominable sin. David makes his infamous faux pas of committing adultery with another man's wife when he should have been on the field of combat (see 2 Sam. 11).

What ensues after this wrongdoing is yet more sin and ultimately death. David spinelessly moves Bathsheba's husband to the front lines so that he is sure to be killed in the fight, which does indeed happen, and the son Bathsheba conceives with David dies only days after being born (see 2 Sam. 12:18). We see that when those who should be setting the moral course for their nations fail to do so, they don't end up saving life, but actually creating more calamity in the process. David belonged on the field, but he was pacified by the palace. When we don't stand up to those who are in the wrong, we run the risk of becoming like them.

I wish I could ask the Neville Chamberlains of today, "If the allied powers would have acted sooner, how many lives that were lost on the battlefield and in the ovens could have been saved while the world sat idle, making up its mind?"

Would the fates of other European countries been different had their monarchs refused to vacate their thrones during the Nazi occupation? The ruling leaders of Poland and Holland for example went into exile. According to estimates, about 3 million of Poland's 3.3 million Jews were killed (91 percent), and 100,000 of 140,000 Jews in the Netherlands (71 percent) fell victim to Hitler's extermination campaign. Contrasted with the less than 100 of the 7,800 Danish Jews who lost their lives under King Christian X, the answer is abundantly clear.[8]

What is certain is that those who stood up for godly convictions made a tremendous difference and saved many lives. The names of Casper and Corrie ten Boom have been passed on to the next generation in the celebrated re-telling of their heroic legacy. No one remembers the nameless cowards who turned them in.

Neutrality is only an illusion. Those who are not for God are against Him, as Jesus Himself said, "He who is not with Me is against Me" (Matt. 12:30a). When the inevitable cannot be put off another minute, and a line is drawn in the sand, everyone will have to choose which side of it they're going to stand on. All of life is a dress rehearsal for these moments of clarity, when spiritual principalities and powers are either bound or released through our fear or our faith.

~ ALL OF LIFE IS A DRESS REHEARSAL
FOR THESE MOMENTS OF CLARITY,
WHEN SPIRITUAL PRINCIPALITIES
AND POWERS ARE EITHER BOUND
OR RELEASED THROUGH OUR
FEAR OR OUR FAITH. ~

As it did for Esther, sooner or later it will come down to what *you* believe. Why not decide now?

How far are we going to let the secularists push us? How far will we let the agenda-driven court system bully us? How far are we going to let the Hollywood moguls stain us? How far will we let the public school systems go to brainwash our children? How far will the radical Islamists' agenda advance before we realize the futility of appeasement? It is time for something to be done, and the somebody to do it is you.

Position your life in such a way that allows God to rise up strong, deep, and firm within your spirit. Become a world changer. Live with an even-though in your spirit. Have an even-though in your spirit that releases you to fulfill the will of God at all costs. When you do, you will find that in addition to being a person of conviction, you will also exhibit great courage.

ENDNOTES

1. http://freedomkeys.com/quotations.htm.

2. Concept originating from *Perpetrators, Victims, Bystanders: The Jewish Catastrophe 1933-1945* by Raul Hilberg (HarperCollins, 1993).

3. http://www.auschwitz.dk/docu/king.htm; accessed 9/10/08.

4. http://www.enotes.com/famous-quotes/an-appeaser-is-one-who-feeds-a-crocodile-hoping-it ;

accessed 8/29/08. Winston Churchill quoted in *Reader's Digest* (Pleasantville, NY; Dec. 1954).

5. Corrie ten Boom with John and Elizabeth Sherrill, *The Hiding Place* (Carmel, NY: Guideposts Associates, Inc, 1971), 13.

6. Ibid.

7. Roosevelt quote from:http:// www.quotedb. com/quotes/1256; accessed 8/24/08.

8. "Jews killed from Poland, Netherlands, Denmark," Source: http://www.historyplace.com /worldwar2/holocaust/h-statistics.htm; accessed 8/27/08.

CHAPTER 10

~

BREAKTHROUGH #4—COURAGE

*Courage is not simply one of the virtues but
the form of every virtue at the testing point....*[1]
—C.S. Lewis

*The world is not dangerous because of
those who do harm but because of those
who look at it without doing anything.*
—Albert Einstein

Little Frodo Baggins shuddered as he lay down to sleep in the eerie woods of Middle Earth. He glanced over at Sam beside him. Was he asleep? Breathing heavily but still restless, as was par for the course on their frightful journey. They were on their way to take the invincible Ring to the place where it was forged—the depths of the darkness of Mount Doom, the only place that its iniquitous power could be undone and destroyed. Frodo himself wondered if he would get any rest at all that night.

A journey of close calls it had been—ringwraiths on their black horses, armies of orcs shrieking as they brandished their weapons, and the watchful Eye of evil that was ever-attempting to track Frodo's progress, to try to seize once again the Ring that was made to rule all others. If Frodo was successful, he would overthrow that great sinister force which had come against hobbits, elves, and men and that had overshadowed the entire land with a foreboding cloud of darkness. *If* he was successful.

They had been on their treacherous journey for what seemed like an eternity, and their destination was still so far off. Frodo was tired of the dreadful cloud of uncertainty he lived under, the terror lurking at every turn. His fingers caressed the weighty Ring hanging around his neck and he suddenly felt nauseous— that familiar mixture of gnawing fear and the penetrating clarity of his mission. How could it be that *he* had been chosen to carry out this most dangerous of assignments?

In spite of the miserable, dank darkness that settled over the land, Frodo found himself thinking of Gandalf, their wise counselor, who must be proud of their journey's slow but sure progress. He smiled to himself as the waning ember of courage began to glow hotter within him. Even he, an insignificant hobbit and an improbable choice for the mission that had been entrusted him, could find somewhere within the courage to go on. After all, ever-faithful Sam was there beside him. Frodo heard a roll of thunder rumble in the distance. Courage. He would need a lot of it. But even though the odds were against them, Frodo just knew that somehow, some way, they were going to make it. They had to.

~

With Mordecai's aid, Esther had awakened to recognize her precarious reality. She made the decision to cry out to the Lord first for help. She had determined who she was and what she really believed. But all of these were precursors to the actual confrontation and the emotional fortitude it would require. Now she would need to add to her character one more attribute: great courage. There was no other way to traverse the treacherous path that lay ahead. The stage before her king had been set, the curtain had been opened, and now it was time for Esther to make that grand entrance—after which there would be no turning back. This was more than a story;

this was the life or death of her people. Esther knew what she must do. The moment she was created for had arrived.

Whether we find ourselves in the imaginary Middle Earth of J.R.R. Tolkien's *Lord of the Rings*, the biblical Persian palace of ancient Susa, or the real world of the 21st century, the theme of courage strikes a chord deep in the human spirit. Movie plots and stories have a way of inspiring us, yet it is imperative that we find a way to translate the emotion we so easily feel in the cinema into the here and now—into the role we have been called to play.

THE SENTIMENT OF COURAGE, THE ADMIRATION OF COURAGE, AND THE RECOGNITION OF COURAGE IN OTHERS ARE ALL VERY DIFFERENT FROM HAVING GENUINE COURAGE OURSELVES.

THE LOST ART OF COURAGE

Once an essential component of daily life, genuine courage seems to be a lost art in America today. Our forebears wouldn't have made it long in the new world without it. Pilgrims on the rocky seas, patriots fighting for the freedom of their fledgling land, pioneers traversing the wild plains. At one time, courage was all but synonymous with the decision to leave everything for an unknown future, and finding the strength of will needed to survive in it.

Since the trauma of World War II, Americans have backpedaled into an essentially safe, comfortable existence that has not had to face an ongoing enemy presence in day-to-day life. But because of this comfort, and because civilian America has never been invaded by a lengthy, multi-national war on its own soil, we have somehow become a nation that speaks of courage—watches movies about courage—but in real life, has had little need of exhibiting courage.

Money, we need. Power? Yes. But courage? We're persuaded we could do without. But what should happen if our back-up plan and 401k's are taken away? What if we really don't have the luxury of safety and security anymore? What if, someday, there is a knock at *our* door? Do we have courage? Do we even know what it is?

It only takes one generation not experiencing something firsthand for it to enter the realm of myth rather than reality. That generation's children grow up thinking of courage as the subject of fictitious bedtime stories rather than the stuff of everyday life.

Spiritually speaking, Christians in Western nations are too often losing courage about their faith, despite how nonthreatening their environments are. While our brothers and sisters around the world are giving their lives for their beliefs, and Muslim young people are strapping bombs to themselves in the name of Allah, we struggle to have a culture of faith strong enough to get our young people to stand around a flag pole one day a year for a few minutes of prayer. We cowered before a few atheists who removed prayer from school. Now prayer is being brought right back in, but not prayer to the God of our forefathers. We were too scared to keep prayer in school, and now we are too scared to keep it out.

WE WERE TOO SCARED TO KEEP PRAYER IN SCHOOL, AND NOW WE ARE TOO SCARED TO KEEP IT OUT.

Indeed, courage in facing outward foes and forces, facing antagonistic, determined enemies, has not been required of the vast majority of 21st century Americans. And what about the need we have for courage as Christians, whatever our nationality? What does the Bible say about the need for valor in the life of the believer? Where does the need for bravery fit into contemporary Christianity?

If you have read even a portion of the Bible, you know that its pages are filled with examples of very real people who faced very real situations that required very real courage. Over and over, God tells His people, individually and corporately, "Fear not!"

Why the need for this command? Because for the majority of humanity, throughout all of time, *there were very legitimate reasons to fear!*

The giants occupying the land of Israel's promise, intimidating the Hebrew spies.

The death threats hissed out at the prophet Elijah by the wicked Queen Jezebel.

The multiple shipwrecks Paul endured on his perilous apostolic journeys.

The hostile warnings from the authorities commanding the disciples not to speak in Jesus' name.

The stones being hurled at Stephen as he gazed toward an open Heaven.

The barbaric Romans, who employed crucifixion as a death penalty for any insurrectionists they deemed a threat to their government.

No matter the era, nothing *anywhere* in Scripture was *ever* accomplished by *anyone* who did not have great courage in the face of genuine (and most times physical) danger. Not just emotional peril or stress or anxiety—real, tangible fear for their lives and the lives of their families.

Why should we be any different? Where does it say that our lives will be exempt from the fights and foes that every generation that has walked in the ways of God has experienced?

Courage then, and great courage at that, is a prerequisite for walking in the purposes of God. Fear must be banished and courage must be embraced.

～ GREAT COURAGE IS A PREREQUISITE FOR WALKING IN THE PURPOSES OF GOD. ～

Our Jewish friends will have an appreciation and understanding of the depth of the Hebrew word for courage, *chazak*, used in Psalm 27: 11-14:

Teach me Your way, O Lord,

And lead me in a smooth path, because of my enemies.

Do not deliver me to the will of my adversaries;
For false witnesses have risen against me,
And such as breathe out violence.

I would have lost heart, unless I had believed
That I would see the goodness of the Lord
In the land of the living.

Wait on the Lord;
Be of good courage [chazak],
And He shall strengthen your heart;
Wait, I say, on the Lord!

Some meanings attributed to the word *chazak* (khaw-zak') are "to fasten upon, to seize, to be strong, to fortify, to bind, to conquer."[2] One commentary on this verse says it this way: "...hope in the Lord, be stouthearted and decided in your convictions, and then God will instill courage to your heart. Interestingly, you first step out in faith, obeying the mitzvah (commandment) to hope in the Lord, and then God causes your heart to be filled with courage (the verb *amets* is *hiphil*, meaning the Lord produces the courage within you."[3]

We in Western civilization have not connected with the need for courage, but we now must recover this lost virtue in our present day, live it, and teach it to our children. Esther had no idea the ramifications her life would hold for successive generations. Similarly, we have no concept of how God desires to place us in exactly the right place at exactly the right time in order to accomplish a crucial feat, which has the potential to change everything. We must be prepared for that moment.

As in Esther's day, Daniel prophesied a time to come when the people of God would have an acute need for godly courage:

> *Those who do wickedly against the covenant he shall corrupt with flattery;* **but the people who know their God shall be strong, and carry out great exploits** (Daniel 11:32).

This verse speaks to me not only of the future but also of today, of the need for a God-fearing company who, *no matter what*, will know their God, will be strong, and will perform courageous acts for the sake of His name. To achieve the Kingdom exploits we were meant to, we must know our God, know our values and convictions, and know what it means to walk the unbending road of courage.

THE FACE OF COURAGE

Elisabeth Elliot had to make an unimaginably painful decision when her 28-year-old husband, Jim, was brutally killed by the Auca natives of the jungles of Ecuador in 1956, along with four other missionaries. If you were in Elizabeth's position, at that point of utter devastation, would you believe that God had called you to that mission field? Or would you think it had all been one big mistake?

165

Elisabeth's bravery led her to take her young daughter, then just a toddler, and go back to the same people who had murdered her husband and bring the good news of the Gospel to them. Many in the tribe came to faith, which is even today being passed down to successive generations. As her husband Jim had stated, and died still believing: "He is no fool who gives what he cannot keep to gain what he cannot lose."[4] This statement, so flawlessly put, is the testimony of courage.

It takes courage to stand against the Hamans of the world. It took courage for Winston Churchill to stand firm against the tide of popular opinion in his day. It took courage for Corrie ten Boom's family to act against the Third Reich and save Jews from Hitler's death camps. It took courage for William Wilberforce to work tirelessly against the abominable slave trade in Britain. It takes courage for our Christian brothers and sisters around the world to stand their ground as they face intense persecution *today* in places like China, Sudan, Afghanistan, Indonesia, and once-Christian Europe.

It takes courage for you and me to count the cost and give ourselves wholly, without reservation, for the Kingdom of God in the morally deluded world we live in. Our own need for courage in the present day is not far off. It is close at hand. Our brothers and sisters worldwide right now are walking through persecution that requires courage of biblical proportions.

The Gaza Strip. A region that has been seized by the terrorist group Hamas and used as a launching pad for endless Qassam rockets shot toward Israeli towns like Sderot. Many times these rockets are purposefully fired from schools and other locations where women and children are found, to force hesitation in the military response from Israeli forces. In addition to the warfare brought into their neighborhoods by this violent vendetta, those living in Gaza must endure the cruel and repressive Shari'ah law imposed by Hamas in their once-quiet communities. Every day they and their families live in an atmosphere of trepidation, dreading the siren's warning of the next attack.

Rami Ayyad, a 26-year-old Arab Christian living in Gaza with his wife, two small children and a third on the way, managed the only Christian bookstore in the Gaza Strip. This alone put his family in danger for the faith that he both believed and practiced. His shop was bombed and he received multiple death threats, ample warning about the grave danger his life was in.

What would you have done? What would I have done? How would we have responded, especially with the responsibility of three small children weighing on us? What stance would we take? Rami decided, "...as for me and my house, we will serve the Lord" (Josh. 24:15b).

In October 2007, just weeks before his third child was born, Rami was kidnapped by Islamic extremists and brutally murdered for daring to defy a tyrannical system.[5]

As is the case in other areas of Israel under Palestinian control—even historic Christian cities like Bethlehem and Nazareth—the Christian population is dwindling dramatically due to hundreds of terrified citizens fleeing their communities. Believers like the pastor of Gaza Baptist Church, Hanna Massad, who was displaced by the violence in his community, have no long-term certainty about their future. "In Gaza, when you say, 'The Lord is my shepherd,' you have to mean it literally. The Lord is the only one who can protect you," said Massad.[6]

What would it be like to be a believer in Gaza in this tumultuous season? How would you respond to the threats circulating around your family? Would you draw the conclusion that the godly thing to do, for the safety of your family, would be to close your shop and silence your witness? Would you give up hope, or continue to persevere?

Think of **Iran** where the ruling dictator Ahmadinejad proposed a law that would impose a death sentence for any Muslim who converts to another religion. Although Christians are protected under the Iranian constitution, they cannot worship freely or hold public office—and they can be arrested for even speaking to Muslims about their faith.

Some, with the courage of their convictions, are leading house churches in Iran, where there have been reports that groups of Muslim converts to Christianity have doubled in size in the last six months.[7] Although the price is high, if these believers do not persevere, what will happen to the testimony of God in the nations in which they live?

> ~ SOME, WITH THE COURAGE OF THEIR CONVICTIONS, ARE LEADING HOUSE CHURCHES IN IRAN, WHERE THERE HAVE BEEN REPORTS THAT GROUPS OF MUSLIM CONVERTS TO CHRISTIANITY HAVE DOUBLED IN SIZE. ~

Then there is **Jerusalem**. On July 2, 2008, a Palestinian construction worker drove a bulldozer through the public streets on a terrorist rampage that left three dead and more than 70 injured. He aimed for Jewish pedestrians and rammed a public bus several times, overturning it.

In an instant, at that moment an Israeli soldier home on leave and an off-duty anti-terror unit police officer ran toward the bulldozer and gunned down the terrorist, who in his last moments yelled "Allah Akhbar!" and stepped on the gas pedal to do as much harm as possible.[8]

But we need not look as far as the Arab world to encounter instances of courage in the face of terror. Consider what is happening in the "free" world.

The Netherlands. Geert Wilders is a Dutch parliamentarian living in a society vastly infiltrated by the ominous, dark cloud of fundamental Islam. Mr. Wilders is also a filmmaker who in 2008 put his reputation on the line by producing the controversial short film, *Fitna* (an Arabic word commonly used to mean division, anarchy, disagreement, or test of faith). Wilders made the movie with the purpose of alerting the Western world to the present dangers brought about by the rise of radical Islam and the bloodshed it is spreading across the Middle East, Europe, and the West.

Wilders has come under incredible backlash for producing this controversial, hard-hitting film, but he has not backed down in his determination to lift his voice. Although he has received much opposition and many death threats for his bold move in taking a stand against Islamists, Mr. Wilders has determined to be one who acts on his convictions by courageously raising an alarm for the cause of truth.

United Kingdom. In one of many such modern-day examples in Great Britain, two adolescent schoolboys in a town outside Manchester, England (a major Muslim stronghold in the West) made a decision to stand up for what they believed.

These two boys, on a normal public school day in their normal lives, were suddenly faced with the requirement of kneeling down and praying to Allah during a mandated exercise in a religious education lesson. They had to decide whether they would, like all the other students, put on the required Muslim headdress to participate in the prayer demanded of them, or whether they would refuse to dishonor the God of Abraham, Isaac, and Jacob.

Like the three Hebrew boys who turned their backs on bowing to the statue, they chose the latter. They received detention for their choice, but undoubtedly have set a precedent for future decisions they will need to make in their lives.[9] By taking a stand, these young boys made a small but weighty statement that they will not bow to the cultural pressures or to fear that would seek to paralyze them in a day when the radical Muslim agenda is extending across the West in nations that have historically been Christian. Though they probably did not fully understand the implications of their decision, these two boys allowed courage to rise up within them and determine their actions. Perhaps it is the young who will teach us the much-needed lessons of courage.

A Rose Ere Blooming

In the midst of the vital call and tremendous need to have great courage in this hour, one more truly remarkable account comes to us from the horrific era of World War II—a simple Christian family that found the strength to uphold their values and to make a lasting statement of *chazak* with their lives.

Today it is widely-accepted that the German public's true and unfortunate legacy during the war lies not in what they did in response to their despotic leader and his horrendous practices, but in what they did *not* do. There were, however, rare and moving exceptions to this tragic trend, which speak of what it means to truly love and obey God and to live with undying courage.

> ~ THE GERMAN PUBLIC'S TRUE AND UNFORTUNATE LEGACY DURING THE WAR LIES NOT IN WHAT THEY DID, BUT IN WHAT THEY DID *NOT* DO. ~

Such a legacy of courage was left by brother and sister, Hans and Sophie Scholl, and members of the White Rose, a resistance movement that challenged the tyrannical regime that had taken over their nation. Compared to the rifles and clubs taken up ruthlessly by their oppressors, their weapons were of a different sort: paper, ink, envelopes, stamps, and a small manually operated duplicating machine they operated aback a courtyard.

Hans and Sophie, in their late teen years when their resistance to Hitler began, chose to brave the repressive ideologies of their day to appeal to the conscience of a nation. They believed that there were many who, behind closed doors, were opposed to what was going on around them, but needed encouragement to step out and speak against the violence. It was this certainty, along with the belief that they were obligated to live for a cause greater than themselves that led them to initiate an antiestablishment leaflet campaign, which, despite its humble means, became notorious to Nazi authorities in that day, and venerated by freedom-loving people in this day.

Hans and Sophie, of their own free will and against the better judgment of their father, had joined the Hitler Youth in their adolescence, but quickly became disenchanted with the programs due to their hate-filled, mind-numbing philosophies. They were Christians and highly literate, self-expressive free-thinkers who chose to distance themselves from the mandatory Nazi organization to pursue other interests, including the reading of literature that had been banned in the already-stifling atmosphere of pre-war Germany.

Hans founded the White Rose with a handful of friends while attending the University of Munich in the early 1940s. Together, they hoped to appeal to the German intelligentsia and more liberal-minded university students with their ultimatum to protest violations of democratic freedom imposed by Hitler and his minions. With the guidance of a cooperating professor, the young people were able to secretly distribute thousands of leaflets throughout southern Germany. At great personal risk, they not only mailed out the pamphlets, but transported them on their own persons from city to city to spread their message of social liberty and passive resistance.

At their young age, they had the wherewithal to ask the question whose answer, in the matter of a few short years, would be known by not just thousands, but millions worldwide:

"Who among us has any conception of the dimensions of shame that will befall us and our children when one day the veil has fallen from our eyes and the most horrible of crimes...reach the light of day?"[10]

Though lauding their bravery, what many accounts fail to mention is the Scholls' firm belief in God that impelled them to pursue the road less traveled. If there were any question as to their belief in the spiritual struggle of the evil against the good, this excerpt describing Hitler from their fourth leaflet should clear up any doubts:

> Every word that comes from Hitler's mouth is a lie. When he says peace, he means war, and when he blasphemously uses the name of the Almighty, he means the power of evil, the fallen angel, Satan. His mouth is the foul-smelling maw of Hell, and his might is at bottom accursed. True, we must conduct a struggle against the National Socialist terrorist state with rational means; but whoever today still doubts the reality, the existence of demonic powers, has failed by a wide margin to understand the metaphysical background of this war. Behind the concrete, the visible events, behind all objective, logical considerations, we find the irrational element: The struggle against the demon, against the servants of the Antichrist.[11]

A janitor saw Hans and Sophie secretly dispersing leaflets on the grounds of the University of Munich campus in February 1943. He called the Gestapo and Hans and Sophie were arrested, just months before the fighting in Europe would come to an end. They and their friend Christopher Probst were immediately tried for high treason, found guilty by the Nazi judge, and executed by guillotine only a few hours later.

Each of the three yet-unsung heroes faced their deaths valiantly. In a meeting they were allowed with each other just before their death sentences were carried out, Christopher consoled his comrades by assuring them, "...in a few minutes we will meet again in eternity." Seconds before Hans laid his head on the block, he shouted in a loud voice his life's epithet, "Long live freedom!"[12]

But it was Sophie, who was first to die, who left the clearest impression. The prison warden's report records it in lucid detail: "She went without batting an eyelash. None of us could understand how such a thing was possible. The executioner said he had never seen anyone die like that."[13] Sophie was able to make good on her observation of only a few days earlier, "With all those people dying for the regime, it is high time that someone died against it."[14]

Though Hitler and is henchmen did all they could to stifle their voice, Hans and Sophie from a higher vantage, ended up having the last word over Hitler. Later in the same year when they were executed, allied forces dropped *over 5 million copies* of their sixth and final leaflet via aircraft over cities such as Cologne and Hamburg. Hans and Sophie's message had become a legacy, reaching more of their fellow countrymen than they could have in ten lifetimes.[15]

The most poignant call to courage, which I find in the heroic life of Sophie Scholl is found in her last words to her mother, who was allowed, along with her husband, to meet with their children shortly before their executions. Sophie's sister relays in her book, *The White Rose*, what those few brief moments between children and parents entailed. Both Hans and Sophie were in the best of spirits, smiling and holding their heads high. They possessed the composure of ones who believed their deaths were not in vain, but rather, would continue the same legacy of altruistic courage their lives had already created.

THEY POSSESSED THE COMPOSURE OF ONES WHO BELIEVED THEIR DEATHS WERE NOT IN VAIN, BUT RATHER, WOULD CONTINUE THE SAME LEGACY OF ALTRUISTIC

~ COURAGE THEIR LIVES HAD
ALREADY CREATED. ~

Wanting to give her daughter some parting words of comfort, her mother whispered, "'Remember Sophie: Jesus.' Gravely, firmly...Sophie replied, 'Yes—but you must remember too.'"[16]

With this, the young woman could have simply been offering her mother that same comfort, stressing how much she would need it after losing two children in one day. But I think the brave social activist was admonishing her mother, who still had time left on this earth, by reminding her that, while we gain comfort by recalling what Jesus did for us, we ourselves must remember Him by living our lives in like manner.

~

As inspired as we feel by this beautiful and epic display of true courage, we need to remember not to despise the day of small beginnings (see Zech. 4:10). Courage is like a seed that must be planted deep in the human spirit, take root, and grow before it blooms into the exquisite rose that wins the favor of all.

Just as Esther declared, "If I perish, I perish," God is asking us to die to our sin, our apathy, our empty lifestyle choices, to our fear of man. It begins by the water cooler. In the classroom. At the family reunion. It begins by wanting to do more with your life than you know is possible, but doing it anyway. I urge you, by the mercies of God (see Rom. 12:1-2) to renounce the entrapments of distraction and denial and to cry out, with conviction, for the kind of courage that makes history.

ENDNOTES

1. http://www.brainyquote.com/quotes/quotes/c/cslewis400196.html.

2. "Chazak," *Biblesoft's New Exhaustive Strong's Numbers and Concordance with Expanded Greek-Hebrew Dictionary.* Copyright © 1994, 2003, 2006 Biblesoft, Inc. and International Bible Translators, Inc.

3. John J. Parsons, "Wait on the Lord—Chazak!"; http://www.hebrew4christians.com/Meditations/Chazak/chazak.html; accessed 8/24/08.

4. Elisabeth Elliot, *Shadow of the Almighty: The Life and Testament of Jim Elliot* (New York: Harper and Brothers, 1958), 15.

5. Deann Alford, "Christian Bookstore Manager Martyred in Gaza City," ChristianityToday.com; http://www.christianitytoday.com/ct/2007/octoberweb-only/141-12.0.html; accessed 8/26/08.

6. Jeremy Weber, "My Heart Is in Gaza," ChristianityToday.com;http://www.christianitytoday.com/ct/2008/april/3.14.html; accessed 8/24/08.

7. Joseph Abrams, "Iran Arrests Suspected Converts to Christianity," FoxNews.com, 5/29/08; http://www.foxnews.com/story/0,2933,359944,00.html; accessed 5/30/08.

8. Yaakov Katz, "He Cried Allah Akhbar and Hit the Gas," *The Jerusalem Post*, 7/2/08; http://www.jpost.com/servlet/Satellite?cid=1214726188722&pagename=JPost%2FJPArticle%2FShowFull; accessed 7/3/08.

9. "Report: Schoolboys Get Detention for Refusing to Pray to Allah," by FoxNews.com; http://www.foxnews.com/story/0,2933,376746, 00.html; accessed 8/26/08.

10. "White Rose Leaflets: Translations of the 6 Printed Leaflets," Holocaust Education & Archive Research Team, http://www.holocaustresearchproject.org/revolt/wrleaflets.html; accessed 8/15/08.

11. Ibid.

12. Hermann Vinke, trans. by Hedwig Pachter, *The Short Life of Sophie Scholl* (New York: Harper and Row, 1984), 188.

13. Ibid.

14. Ibid., 163-164.

15. Katherine Morley, Tim Nunn and Reeling & Writhing, *The Arts & the Holocaust: Lessons From the Past for the Citizens of Today;* http://www.reelingwrithing.com/holocaust/ download.htm, pp. 157-158; accessed 9/1/08.

16. Vinke, *The Short Life of Sophie Scholl*, 187.

CHAPTER 11

~

BREAKTHROUGH #5—
DIVINE STRATEGY

*"You must do the things you
think you cannot do."*
–Eleanor Roosevelt

*So it was, when the king saw Queen Esther standing in the
court, that she found favor in his sight, and the king held
out to Esther the golden scepter that was in his hand. Then
Esther went near and touched the top of the scepter. And
the king said to her, "What do you wish, Queen Esther?
What is your request? It shall be given to you—up to half
the kingdom!" So Esther answered, "If it pleases the king,
let the king and Haman come today to the banquet that I
have prepared for him"* (Esther 5:2-4).

I don't have sufficient adjectives to describe how awe-inspiring I find this part of Esther's story. I marvel and am amazed at
the greatness and wisdom of God evident in this adventure!

Think of it...the fate of Israel hangs in the balance. National destruction is imminent. The situation has never been
darker for the Jews. Total destruction is quickly approaching.

The king's pronouncement, which cannot be reversed, has already been decreed. Death cackles at the doorstep of every Jewish family's home as the hour of execution draws near.

And in the middle of this drama, we have a young, orphan queen. And what is the answer for this cataclysmic catastrophe? What is salvation's strategy? Call an angel? Call a thousand angels? Send fire from Heaven? A plague? The death angel to kill all the firstborn? What is the strategy for supernatural deliverance?

A dinner party.

Better yet, two dinner parties!

Oh, the depth of the riches both of the wisdom and knowledge of God! How unsearchable are His judgments and His ways past finding out! (Romans 11:33)

Esther has recognized the gravity of her situation. She has broken through the defense mechanisms of distraction and denial. She has cried out to the Lord in prayer and called a corporate fast to petition Heaven. She knows she will not compromise or shirk her duty because she has determined her convictions, releasing within her great courage. And now, all that is left is for her to make her move. Her heart has been tested, her priorities established, her identity discovered and secured. Now it is for her to play the part God has written for her in these climactic moments of her script's finale.

And so, Esther sends out the invitations to a dinner party. Just a small affair. Esther, the king, and the man who is trying to kill her.

What Is in Your Hand?

We love the supernatural elements we find in Scripture. God, as Author and Sustainer of the created order, can override it to do whatever He wants—and we like it when He does. How exciting it is when God "does His thing"! We like it when

He makes the sun stand still, an axe head float, turns water into wine, and raises the dead. But we easily forget that the central theme of the whole Bible is how God delights to partner with man. He even respects man as a free agent so much that He endowed him with a free will, requiring that man not only partner with Him, but choose to partner with Him at that.

THE CENTRAL THEME OF THE ENTIRE BIBLE IS HOW GOD DELIGHTS TO PARTNER WITH US.

Throughout Scripture when God does the miraculous, there is always—every time—the need for man to take some practical, natural step of faith to release the supernatural response.

God splits the Red Sea, but Moses has to stretch forth his staff over it.

God demolishes the walls of Jericho, but the Israelites have to march around them for seven days in silence and then lift up a shout.

God causes the Midianites to slay each other before Gideon's army, but not before the leader has to reduce his troops to a mere 300 men.

God continues to fill the widow's jars with flour and oil, but first she has to give her last meal to the prophet.

Jesus feeds 5,000, but the boy has to give his fish and bread to see it multiplied.

Jesus heals the paralytic, but first his friends have to climb up to the roof and lower him down through the ceiling.

The Word reveals a God of relationship who, even more than He desires to deliver His people, desires to be *with* them in the process. And so, using what was in her hand, Esther does what she knew how to do. She humbly, yet gracefully, prepares to wine and dine her beloved, as only she can.

Even so, we don't see a magnificent display of God's grandeur. He doesn't astound anyone with an unexpected 11th-hour appearance accompanied by an incredible outburst of thunder and lightning. No parting of the Red Sea this time! It's still the orphan girl and her aged uncle who remain in the spotlight till the very end. The Jewish people have long since discerned this detail and have incorporated it into their annual festival of remembrance.

Both Passover (the Jewish feast celebrating the Jews' deliverance from Egyptian slavery) and Purim (which celebrates the triumph of Esther) occur in the Hebrew month of Adar. The teaching of the rabbis compares these two holidays and declares that the joy of Purim is greater than the joy of Passover because, in the feast of Purim, the miracle we experience is one that originates from man and is executed by man— by someone just like us. Therefore, Purim gives us great hope and the confidence that we, too, can defeat whatever comes against us.

Think about it: The story of Purim is the story of an orphan girl living in exile. I don't know that you could get much closer to a polar opposite of the almighty, all-powerful, omniscient God of the universe. The fabric of the story is also a stark contrast. Instead of God sending plagues as He did upon Egypt, Esther had to use what was hers (favor with the king) to save her people.

Esther is now the protagonist orchestrating the outcome of her own story. Not only are the actual voice of God, and angels of God, and supernatural miracles of God absent from the Book of Esther, but when her trusted advisor, Mordecai, points out that this is undoubtedly the reason she has come to her royal position, he decides that not even *he* will tell her what to do! Esther strategizes and executes her own plan—right down to the choice of table linens.

God is sovereign, and we can do nothing apart from His Spirit, but did it ever occur to you that (like Esther) maybe, just maybe, God desires to manifest His glorious, perfect, matchless plan through *your* life? That maybe *you* are the Esther this world is waiting for? That probably, almost certainly, you are, at the very least, the Esther that *your* world is waiting for?

~ *YOU* ARE THE ESTHER YOUR ~ WORLD IS WAITING FOR!

Beloved, God does have a divine strategy to change the world we're living in. And for an immediate revelation of what that strategy looks like, put down this book and walk to the nearest mirror!

If you never see an angel, if you never heal the sick or raise the dead, if you never have a mystical vision or hear a voice from Heaven; if you are just a very ordinary, everyday person who realizes you're living in an extraordinary time (and you are willing to say yes to God), then *congratulations!* He can use *you* to save a nation! In a very supernaturally natural way, using whatever comes naturally to you, whatever is in your hand.

IN THE HANDS OF A QUEEN

Esther realizes her moment of action has come. Her one and only beloved family member is under threat of imminent fatality, and she has just learned that her husband has issued a death warrant for her entire nation. After finding out all of this, and the fact that her very life is at stake, what is Esther's reaction? Does she rally an army? Fortify her castle? Hire some henchmen to take care of Haman? (Which, if we're honest, would have been our knee-jerk response.) No. In the face of impending disaster that she knows she alone must single-handedly avert, Esther says, "I know, I'll throw a dinner party!"

What lessons can we learn from her reaction?

For one, move the battle onto your own field, your own terms, not your enemy's.

But also, generally speaking, I think that we in the Body of Christ today are much too apt to dismiss the practical. We tend to think that in order to win our families for God or to make an impact in the lives of our coworkers, we must be caught up in some kind of third heaven encounter. We assume that if God hasn't given us "a word" with 14 confirmations and 1,200 supporting Scriptures, we aren't equipped to move on His behalf. This is simply not the case.

I love the story about how David met his wife, Abigail (see 1 Sam. 25). David had been slighted by an evil man, Nabal, who refused to return the kindness David's men had shown to his in the wilderness.

Nabal was hardheaded and would not listen to his wife. Knowing that her wise words would not get through to him, and that her husband's impudence had put all of their lives in jeopardy, she decided to take care of business herself. An unsupported and uneducated woman, she did not have a lot of resources at her disposal, so she did the one thing she knew how to do. She baked! And guess what? It worked!

She quickly prepared a feast for David and his men, including raisin clusters and fig cakes, which apparently, back then, were all the rage, and she pleaded with him not to slay her and her household because of her husband's obstinacy.

Perhaps the old adage, "A way to a man's heart is through his stomach," is more spiritual than we thought! Sometimes divine strategy is a combination of good manners and a well-timed meal.

One of the young men who has served for about ten years on the Eagles' Wings Ministry team came back recently from his summer vacation, excited about what he witnessed God doing in his hometown.

Many years ago, his mother began anonymously putting groceries on the doorstep of a nearby disadvantaged household where three young children lived. The wife was a new believer and the husband was an alcoholic/drug addict. Through this one woman's faithfulness in continuing to deliver groceries and build relationship with her neighbors, God began to draw this family into fellowship with other believers.

Today, that couple serves as the worship leaders at a growing and vibrant congregation where revival has been breaking out among the young people and impacting the community. Additionally, all three of the couple's children are now living for the Lord.

God moved mightily through this seemingly simple decision that one person made to bless others in a practical way. It turned out to be a divine strategy!

Like the mother in this real-life story, you and I have been deputized by the Holy Spirit to move the Kingdom of God forward right where we are. We have with us (and hopefully inside us) the timeless, matchless, infallible Word of God that provides us with a treasure trove of truth, wisdom, and even first-hand accounts to be inspired by. When you have the law of God etched on your heart and the Spirit of God dwelling inside you, and when you are submitted to the authority He has placed in your life, there are few choices you could make that would result in certain disaster.

Remember: "...[T]he eyes of the Lord run to and fro throughout the whole earth, to show Himself strong on behalf of those whose heart is loyal to Him" (2 Chron. 16:9a).

So Esther hosts a banquet.

A Feast Fit for a King

> Now it happened on the third day that Esther put on her
> royal robes and stood in the inner court of the king's
> palace, across from the king's house, while the king sat on
> his royal throne in the royal house, facing the entrance of
> the house. So it was, when the king saw Queen Esther
> standing in the court, that she found favor in his sight,
> and the king held out to Esther the golden scepter that was
> in his hand. Then Esther went near and touched the top of
> the scepter. And the king said to her, "What do you wish,
> Queen Esther? What is your request? It shall be given to
> you—up to half the kingdom!" So Esther answered, "If it
> pleases the king, let the king and Haman come today to
> the banquet that I have prepared for him." Then the king
> said, "Bring Haman quickly, that he may do as Esther has
> said." So the king and Haman went to the banquet that
> Esther had prepared. At the banquet of wine the king said
> to Esther, "What is your petition? It shall be granted you.
> What is your request, up to half the kingdom? It shall be
> done!" Then Esther answered and said, "My petition and
> request is this: If I have found favor in the sight of the
> king, and if it pleases the king to grant my petition and
> fulfill my request, then let the king and Haman come to
> the banquet which I will prepare for them, and tomorrow
> I will do as the king has said" (Esther 5:1-8).

There are so many amazing things about this account. First,
it is remarkable that Esther had the composure, while staring
complete annihilation in the face, to respond not with hyster-
ics but with holy insight. But here is what else I find most fascinating, a question I believe is worth pondering:

Why does Esther invite Haman to the banquet?

If she has to make a dire appeal to the king, if she has to
plead for his favor and for her life, wouldn't it seem logical to
just request the private audience of her companion alone?
Common sense would say yes.

But what would have happened if, rather than a pleasant, relaxing evening, Esther's message to the king was one of frantic fear and alarm? How would that have rung in his ears? Would she have been perceived as having been just another troublesome wife? Would this sound like just another inter-palace conflict that he, a beleaguered king, would have to sort out?

And suppose Esther didn't have Haman there when she made her case, what would have happened then? Certainly the king would have wanted to meet with Haman privately to talk the matter over with him, and (devious as he was) who knows *what* Haman would say, or what kind of backroom deal he would try to bargain with the king. (Remember, there was money on the line. The deal Haman had made was that the king's treasuries would be strengthened through the Jews' demise.) So if Haman had not been present at the banquet but consulted later, it's very possible that he and the king would have reached a compromise in which Esther (and maybe Mordecai) kept their lives, but the Jewish people were slaughtered.

Along those lines, while Esther's plan may have initially seemed devoid of reason, a closer look into some of the details of the situation make it apparent that a divine strategy was developing beneath the surface.

What we know of King Ahasuerus (and undoubtedly what Esther knew of him) is that he is an impulsive man with a very bad temper. What's more is that he cannot resolve his anger until it is avenged. Think back to the opening of the story when Vashti refuses her husband's request. We're told that he "became very angry and his wrath burned within him" (Esther 1:12 NASB). It was only after he banished her from his presence that his anger subsided (see Esther 2:1).

Also, the king appears to be a very forgetful person, which may be why he likes having records of the goings-on of his kingdom read to him when he cannot sleep. Once he discovers something from the book of chronicles he had forgotten, it weighs on his mind until he does something about it. The first thing the next morning, the king carries out his idea (see Esther 6:1; 4-6).

Esther's unconventional plan would seem to take the king's temperament into account. She knows he is rash, and at the same time prone to forget things that are of no consequence to him. Consequently Esther only had one shot that she could not afford to miss. So perhaps a banquet was the right move after all. But two? Why did she hold two banquets? Why does she put the king off for another day?

Scripture gives no indication that there was any particular reason for this, and my suspicion is that Esther herself did not know the reason. I can imagine her having the second glass of wine poured for Haman and the king, all the while the knot in the pit of her stomach tightening. Everything was going as planned, the king seemed to be enjoying himself and even repeated his offer to grant her her request. Yet Esther could not bring herself to force the words out of her mouth. Whether it was a case of nerves or just that "knowing" in her "knower" that told her the timing just wasn't right, we're not told she does anything differently the second time. So why the delay?

Whether or not it was part of Esther's original design, the few hours between her first and second banquets are some of the most important in the whole book. Unbeknownst to Esther, a lot was going on behind the scenes. If you'll notice, the events of the story seem to pick up pace and take on a different tone from this point forward.

On his way home from the first banquet, Haman sees Mordecai and is reminded of how much he detests him. It is then that he, along with his wife and friends, hatch the scheme of building a gallows for the man to hang him on the next day. However, when Haman goes to the king the next morning to get him to approve his idea, he doesn't even have the chance to say the words.

Largely due to his own pride (now greatly stoked after being invited to a private gathering with the king and queen),

Haman ends up in the most humiliating of circumstances: honoring the very man he hoped to kill. Someone will be hung on the gallows he built the day before, but it isn't Mordecai.

Haman essentially digs his own grave, but what is it that causes the king to not be able to fall asleep the night after the first banquet? (It is during this time that he is reminded of how Mordecai had saved his life and had not received any recompense for this deed.) Was it coincidence, or providence? A lucky break, or the unseen hand of God? God has a subtle way of showing those with eyes to see that, no matter how absent He may seem, He is working, moving, shaping, directing.

Esther's second banquet makes me think of a well-known Scripture:

> *You prepare a table before me in the presence of my enemies...* (Psalm 23:5).

It was God's table Esther had come to. Without her knowledge, God was setting everything up for a victory far more comprehensive than she even had in mind. What makes the turn of events all the more brilliant is not only the apparent irony of the affair, but the paradoxical element built into the very framework of Haman's scheme.

GOD WAS SETTING EVERYTHING UP FOR A VICTORY FAR MORE COMPREHENSIVE THAN ESTHER HAD IN MIND.

Haman was an Amalekite, which not only meant he hated the Jews, but that he did not believe in the goodness of God—or any god. The Amalekites were fatalistic; they believed that no one held any power to change what had been destined for them by "life"; that everyone's fate occurred by chance and not by design. To demonstrate this, Haman cast lots (*pur*) to determine on which date he would arrange for the destruction of the Jews.

The chance episode of insomnia, which the king experienced the night before Haman was to implement his vindictive plot, to me seems like God getting the last laugh. The "coincidental" incident makes a definitive comment on Who is running the show.

> *The king's heart is in the hand of the Lord, like the rivers of water; He turns it wherever He wishes* (Proverbs 21:1).

Although there were many facets to Esther's strategy in how she approached the predicament, here is the key: Esther did not bring her *problem* to the king. Instead she brought him esteem, consideration, honor, submission. Every time she addresses the king, she posits her request in terms of what will please and honor the king. "[I]f it pleases the king...I will do as the king has said..." (Esther 5:8). Her language is a language of selflessness and respect.

Esther realizes that the threat is so complex she cannot just enter into a political dialogue with the king. She cannot begin a series of lengthy negotiations. She needs to touch his heart. She needs to stir his emotions. She needs to rouse his love for her and his zeal to protect her. To do this, Haman (the threat) has to be in close range.

But here is the thing that Esther realized: even with the enemy seated right at her table, it doesn't matter how sinister, evil, dangerous, or present the enemy seems to be, ultimately, her life—and indeed our lives, our futures—are in the hands of the King.

~ ESTHER DOES NOT SECURE HER VICTORY BY ENGAGING HER ENEMY, BUT BY ENTERTAINING HER KING. ~

And so Esther's focus, remarkably, is not on the threats of Haman, but on the supremacy of her king. Esther does not secure her victory by engaging her enemy, but by entertaining her king.

RECOGNIZING THE REALITY

You'll remember that Esther's foremost breakthrough was when she recognized the reality of her situation and chose to do something about it. We too need to disentangle ourselves from our own defense mechanisms of distraction and denial, and grasp that there is a very real, very dangerous, very imminent threat upon us. But at the same time, we cannot neglect to recognize another truth, which Esther again illustrates for us so poignantly. We cannot forget the definitive reality of the authority of our Sovereign King. Esther sat at the feet of her king, full of adoration and reverence, realizing that nothing was needed for her deliverance but his favor.

In these turbulent days, we need to keep one solitary focus upon the, "God and Father of all, who is over all and through all and in all" (Eph. 4:6 NIV). We need to respectfully sit at His feet, gaze into His eyes, and honor Him as the One True and Living God who is and always will be King of kings and Lord of lords. We need to prepare a banquet for our King. Even with the enemy at the door, we need to know that God, our Great King, is still on His throne.

An old Pentecostal evangelist used to say, "You don't have any problems. All you need is faith in God." Simplistic maybe, but so true. Whether God calms the storm around you, or calms you in the midst of the storm, the outcome is still the same. We are safe in His love. We are invited to His banqueting table where He comforts us. Even—maybe especially—in the presence of our enemies.

CHAPTER 12

~

FOR SUCH A TIME AS THIS

"...There is no nation on earth powerful enough to accomplish our overthrow. Our destruction, should it ever come at all, will be from another quarter. From the inattention of the people to the concerns of their government, from their carelessness and negligence."

—Daniel Webster

"Israel is a rotten, dried tree that will be annihilated in one storm." –President Mahmoud Ahmadinejad, head of the now-nuclear Iran

A Muslim cab driver confessed to murdering his 16-year-old daughter in cold blood because she refused to wear a hajib (traditional Muslim head scarf). She was found by police lying motionless on her bedroom floor and died under emergency care several hours later.[1]

After a late-night heated argument, an enraged father strangled his grown daughter in their own home for refusing to submit to an arranged marriage.[2]

Within months of these incidents, a husband and father of four was arrested for murdering his wife and daughters because they did not live up to his expectation of Muslim women.

191

He killed them by pouring gasoline over them in their sleep and setting them on fire.[3]

"Honor killings," as they are referred to in many Islamic cultures, are commonplace and even legalized in nations such as Egypt, Syria, and Morocco.[4] Under Shari'ah law, men are permitted, and even encouraged to avenge any acts deemed dishonoring to their families by whatever means necessary. What to us sounds like the heinous deeds of the mentally deranged, for others, is an accepted and completely respectable expression of faith.

As you read these stories, you're probably picturing the crimes taking place in an Eastern Arab context like Saudi Arabia or Jordan, places that have long been strangleholds of Islamic fundamentalists' rule. It may surprise you to learn that these murders took place in developed, Western, democratic nations (Ontario, Canada; Atlanta, Georgia, USA; and London, England, to be specific). These cases and others speak to the growing reality of extremist Muslim hate practices that are endangering many lives in the civilized world.

In August 2008 a Pakistani lawmaker defended the recent "honor killing" of five women in a conservative southwest province. The tribesmen captured the women, beat them, shot them, and then buried them while they were still alive. Their crime? Wanting to marry husbands of their own choosing. The Pakistani representing the murderers described such honor killings as "centuries-old traditions" which need to be carried into the 21st century. He clarified, "Only those who indulge in immoral acts should be afraid."[5]

The unthinkable is now hard not to think about; and instead of being somewhere "over there" it is here. Right here. Right at the door. All the while, a Western world, sedated by moral relativism and network television sits by, scratching its head, afraid to transgress self-imposed stringents of political correctness; too rationally impotent to effectively address the issue, and too morally warped to care.

Now consider these instances from within the American Church that took place in the same years as the above mentioned murders:

"By calling ourselves progressive, we mean we are Christians who recognize the faithfulness of other people who have other names for the way to God's realm, and acknowledge that their ways are true for them, as our ways are true for us."

—Taken from a "welcome statement"
for churches participating in
"Pluralism Sunday," a celebration of
"our interfaith world" sponsored by the Center for
Progressive Christianity.
Organizers state that progressive Christians "thank
God for religious diversity! We don't claim that our
religion is superior to all others." The event will
occur on Pentecost Sunday....[6]

"'Lord' has become a loaded word conveying hierarchical power over things, which in what we have recorded in our sacred texts, is not who Jesus understood Himself to be."

—*The Rev. Susan Anderson-Smith, associate
rector at St. Philips in the Hills Episcopal Church
in Tucson, AZ. Anderson-Smith is quoted in an article in
the* **Arizona Daily Star** *explaining why the use of the
term "Lord" is being restricted at her church.*[7]

"The death, birth and miracle narratives about Jesus of Nazareth are almost certainly confections that emerged from the collective imagination of late first-century C.E. communities of Jews and Gentiles, which had found common ground in a devotion to the ethical teachings of an itinerant street preacher from Galilee. It was apparently the radically countercultural nature of that teaching—as in 'love your enemy'—that set Jesus apart from the countless other street preachers of the time, who may have been something like the first-century version of today's pundits and talk-show hosts."

—*The Rev. Harry T. Cook,*
an Episcopal rector of St. Andrew's
Church in Clawson, MI, in a 2/21/08
Detroit News *commentary.*[8]

All these outrageous quotes may seem totally unrelated to the "honor" killings and other militant acts of religious violence we've discussed, but we need to begin to see the connection. The Church is eroding from the inside out, and a radicalized Islam is encroaching from the outside in. We are losing everything our ancestors fought and died to give us, and we have no one to blame but ourselves.

~ THE CHURCH IS ERODING FROM THE INSIDE OUT, AND A RADICALIZED ISLAM IS ENCROACHING FROM THE OUTSIDE IN. ~

WHAT TIME IS IT?

It was a weekday summer morning in Hertfordshire, England, shortly after 8 A.M. when 53-year-old Susan Levy, a wife and mother active in her local Jewish community, left for work, traveling with her 23-year-old son Jamie during their typical weekly schedule in their hometown north of London. From a close-knit family, Susan and Jamie usually traveled the first leg of their journey together as she went to her job as a legal secretary. Along with her husband, Harry, and her older son Daniel, 25, their family of four was known for enjoying each other's company, reportedly, "doing everything together." [9]

Traveling by train that Thursday, Susan parted ways with Jamie at the Finsbury Park stop, where he got off and she continued on the Piccadilly line toward London. Jaime didn't know that the goodbye he said to his mother that morning would be their last. Her train was destroyed by a detonated bomb at 8:50 A.M. as it passed underneath Russell Square. Simultaneously, two other trains exploded at different locations in London, and about an hour later a double-decker bus blew up at Tavistock Square.[10] The joint attack killing over 50 morning commuters and injuring more than 700 others in London on July 7, 2005, shook a British population to its core.[11]

You may be picturing a video-recording of Osama bin Laden, or other Islamic warlord, who masterminded these attacks from a cave in Afghanistan. What you probably aren't expecting to hear is that the perpetrators of the London bombings had non-remarkable Western upbringings, and three out of the four were second-generation British citizens with secular backgrounds. One, an avid cricket player, owned a $200,000 estate and drove a Mercedes.[12]

In addition to tea and crumpets, the Queen's land is now producing her very own terrorists. But the United Kingdom isn't the only state in the free world that can lay claim to the accomplishment of home-grown terrorism. There's an al-Qaeda training school just outside our nation's capital in Washington, DC.

In the rolling hills of Falls Church, Virginia lies the Islamic Saudi Academy, an Arabic-English-speaking private school owned and funded by Saudi Arabian dollars. The institution has long been under investigation for use of textbooks using intolerant language and has since come under fire for allegedly teaching doctrines such as the permissiveness of killing non-Muslims, or even non-Sunni Muslims. Not long ago, Ahmed Abu Ali, a graduate of the school, was arrested for attempting to launch an al-Qaeda cell in the United States, and participating in an assassination plot against the President.[13]

If you're thinking that Ali may have been the "black sheep" of his peers and not representative of the school's culture and value system, consider this: he graduated as class valedictorian.

Contrast Ali's non-p.c. education with that of middle school students in Amherst, New Hampshire, where a full-out interactive "Saudi Awareness Day" was hosted in May 2007. As part of their public school education, students were taught to carry out religious and cultural customs, such as how to pray directionally to Mecca, men's and women's roles under Saudi culture, and Arabic books and games. The children dressed in appropriate Saudi garb and acted out all the main aspects themselves.[14]

These examples of Muslim infiltration into the mainstream have become the norm, as we seek to sensitize our children to a culture that is anything but sensitive to our own.

A PEOPLE WITHOUT A MORAL COMPASS

Meanwhile, as this is happening in the American education system, the Church is losing its young people. Because we have lowered the standard of what it means to be a Christian, we have become a people without a moral compass, in most respects no different than unbelievers. After proclaiming our faith is no better than any other (see above note on "Pluralism Sunday") our young people seem to be taking our words at face value, and leaving the Church in droves.

Christian research expert George Barna, after years of studying the Western Church, has shown that "less than one out of every ten Christians age eighteen or older believes that absolute moral truth exists."[15] Statistics in the American Church for divorce rates, everyday entertainment habits, and use of medications for depression are essentially identical to those of non-Christians.[16]

"...LESS THAN ONE OUT OF EVERY TEN CHRISTIANS AGE EIGHTEEN OR OLDER BELIEVES THAT ABSOLUTE MORAL TRUTH EXISTS."

Once respected as the bedrock of American society, Christianity has been marginalized and censured for its alleged "intolerance" (at the hands of intolerant, radical secularists). But how much of this have we brought on ourselves because we have been satisfied with being relegated to a subculture rather than engaging our society and transforming it by our influence? If the *salt* loses its *saltiness*, eventually the whole dish will rot. We are exhorted in Scripture to act as a preservative not just for our own sake, but for the good of society at large.

Consider these further comparisons...

In 2008, Tyson Foods allowed persistent Muslim workers at their large plant in Shelbyville, Tennessee, to exchange the Muslim holiday Eid al-Fitr (which marks the end of Ramadan), as a paid holiday in place of Labor Day. This development was achieved after negotiations through the labor union of which the workers are members. The Muslim workers were also granted two prayer rooms for ongoing use to carry out their daily prayers and religious observances, in fulfilling their personal commitment to bowing in prayer five times a day.[17]

When is the last time you've heard of the average Christian praying five times a day...or at all?

Less than 10 percent of families who attend church worship or pray together outside of a weekly service and "the same minimal numbers study the Bible together at home or work together to address the needs of disadvantaged people in their community."[18]

In addition, in this prayer-malnourished society, according to American Values, "Children in the U.S. are now three times

197

as likely to grow up in a single-parent household as they were in 1960, and over 12 million children now live with a never-married parent. In addition, over half of marriages result in divorce—60 percent of which involve children."[19]

While Muslim children are being raised in a culture of disciplined prayer, Christian children are often growing up in broken homes that place as little value on spiritual virtue as they do on marital faithfulness.

In the financial realm, it is widely accepted by analysts and government officials that Saudi Arabia is a large funds supplier for world terrorism, naturally bolstered by the drastic rise in global oil prices. Says the *Times Online*, "[W]ealthy Saudis remain the chief financiers of worldwide terror networks. 'If I could somehow snap my fingers and cut off the funding from one country, it would be Saudi Arabia,' said Stuart Levey, the US Treasury official in charge of tracking terror financing."[20] Apparently, Muslims take seriously the command of giving *zakat* (a portion of one's earnings) to the poor or donating to causes deemed pleasing to Allah.

In light of this, consider America where according to Barna's research, *less than 10 percent* of Christians who attend church give a tithe of their income (10 percent or more) to churches or other Christian organizations.[21] This amounts to millions of dollars every year that is held back from much-needed use in God's Kingdom.

Think of all the educational programs, mission outreaches, and humanitarian aid projects we could be changing the world with if we put our money where our mouths are. Instead, we see a well-financed Muslim elite depriving their people of a basic standard of living (and blaming it on Western capitalist greed) and using that money to incite them to terrorize those whom they have been taught are their enemies.

~ THINK OF ALL THE EDUCATIONAL PROGRAMS, MISSION OUTREACHES, AND HUMANITARIAN AID PROJECTS WE COULD BE CHANGING THE WORLD WITH IF WE PUT OUR MONEY WHERE OUR MOUTHS ARE. ~

In predominantly Muslim regions of the world, data from the United Nations reveals that, in northern Africa, the Middle East, and Asia, fertility rates average at 4 children or more per woman in many nations (and nearly 7 per woman in a nation like Afghanistan); whereas in the United States the fertility rate is 2 per woman (which only maintains the current population). Europe as a whole is in a declining rate, less than 2.0 in nearly every nation of the continent, which makes it extremely vulnerable to the power of Muslim immigration for changing the demographics of the population.[22]

Culturally, in contemporary Western Christianity, we have seen not only a de-emphasis on the family and the importance of raising children, but also the drastic moral decline evidenced by the number of abortions in our nation. As of 2004, 44 million abortions had been performed in the United States, with an average of about 1 million being added each year.[23] Is it any wonder that our testimony is in danger of being lost in this generation if we are not giving the next generation a chance to live?

Europe, unless there is a massive spiritual awakening, will be a Muslim territory in a relatively short matter of time. Islam is flooding Eastern and Western Europe in numbers unprecedented since the height of the Ottoman Empire. This has given geo-political experts cause for serious concern as they ponder the developments of a continent that is more often than not referred to as "Eurabia" to describe its new ethnic composition.

Here are the sobering statistics:

- The birth rate among Muslim Europeans is three times higher than that of non-Muslims.

- The Muslim population in the European Union doubled from 1995 to 2005.[24]

- Experts have predicted a doubling of the Muslim population in Europe in the 20 years between 2005 and 2025.[25]

With this influx in the Muslim population in Europe has come the radicalized sectors of Islam which have purposed to take over the entire continent—and beyond—by forced submission to Allah. Led by the anti-Western speeches of clerics, imams, and terrorist organizers around the world, Israel is bombarded daily with existential threats to her very being, such as those from Mahmoud Ahmadinejad: "Israel is a tyrannical regime that will one day be destroyed," and, "Anybody who recognizes Israel will burn in the fire of the Islamic nation's fury."[26]

Islam has set out to create an empire that includes not just Israel and the Middle East, but Europe and the Americas as well. By mobilizing the native-born populations of Western countries for acts of terrorism as have been discussed, radical Islam seeks to train a growing, radicalized contingent of jihadist Muslims within Western nations to accomplish a terror-wrought transformation from the inside out. As Robert S. Leiken, director of the Immigration and National Security Program concurs, "Europe's emerging mujahideen [Muslim jihadist fighters] endanger the entire Western world."[27]

ISLAM HAS SET OUT TO CREATE AN EMPIRE THAT INCLUDES NOT JUST ISRAEL AND THE MIDDLE EAST, BUT EUROPE AND THE AMERICAS AS WELL.

From the United Kingdom, where London has been nick-named "Londonistan" for its drastic cultural and political swing toward Islam; to Berlin, where churches sit empty and mosques spring up across the landscape, the fabric of Judeo-Christian European culture is deteriorating at an alarming rate.

PREACHING TO THE CHOIR

Some of the most courageous voices speaking out in this culture war raging today are not coming from within the Church, but from some rather unexpected sources.

Italian native Oriana Fallaci, though an avowed atheist, nevertheless demonstrated Mordecai-like characteristics that propelled her into the spotlight as a controversial journalist, speaker, and author. Although her life was cut short after a battle with breast cancer in 2006, she dedicated roughly the last decade of her life to opposing the brutality and fanatical intolerance of radical Islam. Incensed over the 2001 attacks on the World Trade Center, she blamed the leniency and con-ceit of Western intelligentsia for not denouncing the hateful, cowardly actions of terrorists in her scathing critique of the Islamic agenda, *The Rage and the Pride.*

Referred to by one reporter as "the journalist to whom virtually no world figure would say no,"[28] she was known for tackling issues and world leaders head-on, interviewing such figures as Ayatollah Khomeini of Iran, U.S. foreign affairs au-thority Henry Kissinger, Israeli Prime Minister Golda Meir, PLO chief Yasir Arafat, and Prime Minister Zulfikar Ali Bhutto of Pakistan.

Fallaci risked her own life to unequivocally condemn the radicalized contingent taking over her country and became, in the words of David Horowitz, a "warrior in the cause of human freedom."[29]

Bat Ye'or, a respected writer and scholar on the subject of Muslim infiltration and jihad against Israel and the West, was born in Egypt to Jewish parents and later moved with them to Britain when they all were forced out of the country. She has become an authority on the subjects of *Eurabia*, a term that she helped to principally develop, and *dhimmitude*, referring to the subjugation of non-Muslims under Shari'ah law. One of her most influential books is *The Decline of Eastern Christianity Under Islam: From Jihad to Dhimmitude.*

Not a religious woman, Bat Ye'or has been an exemplary voice alerting people everywhere to recognize Islam for what it is. Those who chock the warnings of pastors and Christian leaders up to the politics of religious interest have a tough time explaining away cogent voices like these from outside "the four walls" of the Church.

Another outspoken activist raising awareness about the dangers imposed on Western societies by the fundamentalist, anti-Semitic regime is 1960s sex-icon Brigitte Bardot. Her secular perspective might make her an unlikely candidate for the job, but she has recognized the fallacy of trying to make peace with those who do not want peace, and has thus unapologetically criticized Islamofascism. She has been arrested, fined, and publicly censured for her comments and that, in the liberal, anything-goes courts of Europe. Her questionable methods are nevertheless taking a stand against what she regrets is the 'Islamisation of France.'[30]

May I ask you frankly, if one of the world's most recognized sex-symbols has the wherewithal to identify and morally oppose a totalitarian threat, how much more should we, who have the benefit of knowing God's voice and the Scriptures? Aren't the people of faith the ones who are supposed to be leading the way in the battle for truth and righteousness?

But contrast the firm stance that advocates from the secular arena are taking on this issue with these feeble and ineffective positions taken by those within the Church:

"Europe is suffering because [Christians] do not know how to talk with Muslims. Africa is also having problems

202

on how to talk to Muslims. Ecology is the way to speak to the Muslims because we share the environment."

—The Rev. Munib Younan, bishop of the Evangelical Lutheran Church in Jordan and the Holy Land, addressing a gathering of the Lutheran World Federation[31]

"God doesn't really care how we address Him."

—Catholic Bishop Martinus "Tiny" Muskens of the Netherlands, suggesting on the Dutch television show Network that Christians begin referring to God as "Allah" in an attempt to foster better relations with Muslims. Bishop Muskens predicts that within 100-200 years, Roman Catholics will be addressing prayers to Allah.[32]

While some "religious" leaders like these are engaging in every kind of compromise, demonstrating a terrifying lack of clear moral conviction, it is time for the Church (everyday, ordinary people like you and me) to stand and be counted. It is time for us to realize that, though we may not stand behind microphones, we can become trumpets nonetheless.

OUR FINEST HOUR

Earlier I shared about Viktor Frankl, the Austrian psychologist who was interned at a concentration camp during World War II and who exhorted people encountering extreme duress to overcome by exhibiting moral courage and personal responsibility.

In his book, *Man's Search for Meaning*, Frankl shares the following insight he and his fellow prisoners came to terms with in handling the unforeseen and inopportune circumstances they faced:

We had to learn...that it did not really matter what we expected from life, but rather what life expected from us. We needed to stop asking about the meaning of life, and instead to think of ourselves as those who were being questioned by life—daily and hourly.[33]

You may wish you had never read this chapter. If it's any consolation, I wish there wasn't the need for me to have written it. But we must—each of us—realize that simply by virtue of the time into which we have been born, we have been thrust into the center of an ancient battle that is building to its long-awaited climax by the second.

Perhaps this is not what we thought we would have to be dealing with when we chose our careers, when we got married, when we started saving for retirement. But life isn't always about what you choose; more often than not, it's about what chooses you.

~ LIFE ISN'T ALWAYS ABOUT WHAT YOU CHOOSE; MORE OFTEN THAN NOT, IT'S ABOUT WHAT CHOOSES YOU. ~

Beloved, *what is our day and hour asking of us?*

Gary Bauer, founder of American Values and well-known and respected conservative spokesperson, draws the following conclusion:

> Our enemy believes Americans are decadent, reckless, sex-obsessed and lazy. They see a spiral of plummeting birth rates and soaring abortion rates and think we are ready to die. They see a powerful civilization weakened by secularism and multiculturalism. ...Our enemy thinks we are no longer able to produce the men and women we saw in the fields of Gettysburg, on the beaches of Normandy and in the skies over Vietnam. But I do not believe we are the people our enemy says we are. My hope

and belief is that our enemy has underestimated what America is.[34]

I hope so too.

We have heard the facts—we have seen what is happening on our watch. As believers, the disparity between our callings and our daily lives is all too apparent. And now, we must act.

The hour is late; it is almost too late, unless—somehow—Esther awakens.

ENDNOTES

1. "Man Charged With Killing Daughter in Headscarf Dispute," USAToday.com, Dec. 12, 2007, http://www.usatoday.com/news/world/2007-12-12-canada-headscarfmurder_N.htm; accessed 9/1/08. And "Dad Charged After Daughter Killed in Clash Over Hijab," Dec. 11, 2007, http://www.nationalpost.com/story.html?id=159480.

2. http://www.chicagotribune.com/news/nationworld/chi-arranged-marriage-killingjul08,0,7581978.story?track=rss.

3. http://www.independent.co.uk/news/uk/crime/muslim-husband-who-killed-his-wife-and-children-because-of-their-western-ways-437199.html.

4. http://en.wikipedia.org/wiki/Honor_killing; accessed 9/5/08.

5. http://www.msnbc.msn.com/id/26469519/; accessed 9/8/08.

6. The Institute on Religion and Democracy; http://www.theird.org/NETCOMMUNITY/Page.aspx?pid=533&srcid=183.

7. The Institute on Religion and Democracy; http://www.theird.org/NETCOMMUNITY/Page.aspx?pid=508&srcid=133.

8. The Institute on Religion and Democracy; http://www.theird.org/NETCOMMUNITY/Page.aspx?pid=511&srcid=198.

9. "Obituary: Susan Levy," BBC News, Aug. 3, 2005, http://news.bbc.co.uk/2/shared/spl/hi/uk/05/london_blasts/what_happened/html/default.stm; accessed 9/2/08.

10. "7 July Bombings: Overview," BBC News, http://news.bbc.co.uk/2/shared/spl/hi/uk/05/london_blasts/what_happened/html/default.stm; accessed 9/2/08.

11. England bombing: "Radicalization in the West: The Homegrown Threat," Mitchell D. Silber and Arvin Bhatt for NYPD Intelligence Division, 2007,http://www.investigativeproject.org/documents/testimony/344.pdf, pp. 25-26; accessed 9/1/08.

12. Ibid., 26.

13. "Student Convicted in Plot to Assassinate President Bush," Foxnews.com, Nov. 23, 2005, http://www.foxnews.com/story/0,2933,176409,00.html; accessed 9/2/08.

And "State Dept. Stands Alone on Virginia Saudi School," by The Investigative Project on Terrorism, June 26, 2008, http://www.investigativeproject.org/article/697; accessed 9/1/08.

14. "'Open Tent' at Amherst Middle School," Cabinet.com,http://www.cabinet.com/apps/pbcs.dll/article?AID=/20070531/MILFORD01/70531004/-1/Milford01; accessed 9/1/08.

15. George Barna, Revolution (Wheaton, IL: Tyndale House, 2005), 32.

16. George Barna, The Second Coming of the Church (Nashville, TN: Word Publishing, 1998), 6.

17. "Tyson Plant Drops Labor Day for Muslim Holiday," Foxnews.com, Aug. 5, 2008, http://www.foxnews.com/story/0,2933,397645,00.html; accessed 8/26/08.

18. Barna, *Revolution*, 35.

19. "Marriage and Family," by American Values, http://www.amvalues.org/marriage.php; accessed 9/2/08.

20. Nick Fielding and Sarah Baxter, "Saudi Arabia Is Hub of World Terror," TimesOnline, November 4, 2007, http://www.timesonline.co.uk/tol/news/world/middle_east/article2801017.ece; accessed 9/2/08.

21. Barna, *Revolution*, 33.

22. "Fertility Rates (Children per Family): World Statistics,"http://www.pregnantpause.org/numbers/fertility.htm; accessed 9/2/08.

23. "Abortion Statistics," by Carrie Gordon Earll, http://www.citizenlink.org/FOSI/bioethics/abortion/A000002160.cfm; accessed 9/2/08.

24. "EUROPE: Integrating Islam," by Esther Pan, Council on Foreign Relations, July 13, 2005;

http://www.cfr.org/publication/8252/europe. html; accessed 9/2/08.

25. "Europe's Angry Muslims," by Robert S. Leiken, *Foreign Affairs*, July/August 2005, http://www.foreignaffairs.org/20050701faessay 84409-p0/robert-s-leiken/europe-s-angry-mus- lims.html; accessed 9/2/08.

26. "Ahmadinejad Quotes," May 16, 2006, jpost.com, http://www.jpost.com/servlet/Satel lite?cid=1145961353170&pagename=JPost/ JPArticle/ShowFull; accessed 8/30/08.

27. Leiken, "Europe's Angry Muslims."

28. Quoted in "Oriana Fallaci: Journalist, inter- viewer and author," by Giselle Fernandez, http://www.giselle.com/oriana.html; accessed 9/3/08.

29. "Fallaci: Warrior in the Cause of Human Freedom," by Robert Spencer, FrontPage Magazine.com, Nov. 30, 2005,http://www.front pagemag.com/Articles/Printable. aspx?GUID=CE390DFD-ECC2-4FD1-9E50- 692188922BF7; accessed 9/3/08.

30. "Brigitte Bardot on Trial for Racism," AOL Canada, Apr. 16, 2008,http://entertainment. aol.ca/article/Brigitte Bardot-on-Trial-forRacism /196934/; accessed 9/3/08.

31. Institute on Religion and Democracy; http ://www.theird.org/NETCOMMUNITY/ Page.aspx?pid=533&srcid=183.

32. Institute on Religion and Democracy; http://www.theird.org/NETCOMMUNITY/ Page.aspx?pid=508&srcid=533.

33. Viktor Frankl, *Man's Search for Meaning* (Boston: Beacon Press, 2006), 77.

34. Gary L. Bauer, "Two Battles, One War! Fighting for the Soul of a Nation," March-April 2008, *KAIROS Magazine,* an Eagles' Wings publication.

CHAPTER 13

~

BECOMING AN ESTHER GENERATION

People who fight may lose. People who
do not fight have already lost.[1]
—Bertold Brecht

Benazir Bhutto was 54 years of age when she was killed in a combined shooting and bombing attack on the teeming streets of her native Pakistan.

As I see the terrible incident replayed on screen, and as I see her face on the cover of books, I'm left wondering, *At what point in her life did she realize her destiny was not as a spectator, but as a principal player in her nation's future?* At what point, as she was sipping tea in a posh, metropolitan apartment on the picturesque streets of London, did she say to herself, *I must go back now.*

What makes a person change the course of their life?

What moment defines or re-defines a person's individual journey?

At what point did Dietrich Bonhoeffer know he had to stand against the Third Reich by establishing a church not controlled by their corrupt political agenda? At what point did Winston Churchill decide to give his every waking moment to deterring the malevolent aspirations of a despotic madman? What made the ten Boom family choose to risk their own lives to help people they didn't know escape an untimely death?

At what point did Esther accept that she was the one who was called to stand between her people and complete obliteration? What made her say yes?

Were these choices the product of a gradually growing awareness, or was there a tipping point—a moment of illumination along the way? When and how does the soul shift from the disinterest of an onlooker to the passionate commitment of an avid participant?

How do you awaken a soul?

For Good and Ill

If you'll remember back to the first chapter of our journey, we considered at length how one life really can and does make a difference. We looked at many examples of ordinary people who made an extraordinary impact in their worlds. We also saw how the power of human choice could be used for both good and ill.

I am continually undone by the relentless advance of global terrorism. We're now no longer shocked to hear of another bus exploding, a car bomb detonating, an aircraft scare.

What makes this possible? What kind of psychological preparation is required to produce a suicide bomber? What is their "moment of no return"? When they first volunteer for the assignment? When they finally strap the bombs to their chest? What makes them say yes?

Whether or not we are making what we feel is a huge difference in the world around us, we are contributing to the state of the whole to one degree or another. Everyone, either by what they choose to do or choose not to do, is part of the equation producing the result of our current reality. We are either part of the audience or part of the cast; part of the crowd or part of the force. We are either awake or asleep.

> WHETHER OR NOT WE ARE MAKING WHAT WE FEEL IS A HUGE DIFFERENCE IN THE WORLD AROUND US, WE ARE CONTRIBUTING TO THE STATE OF THE WHOLE TO ONE DEGREE OR ANOTHER.

Mordecai's quandary, as he approached Esther with their predicament, was: How does one awaken a queen who is living in peace, luxury, and comfort? How do you get someone to accept a fact they don't want to believe?

AWAKENING A QUEEN

Mordecai doesn't take Esther's initial protest of why she can't be of help for an answer. He comes back to her with a strong rebuff that restated the matter point-blank.

> *Then Mordecai told them to reply to Esther, "Do not imagine that you in the king's palace can escape any more than all the Jews. For if you remain silent at this time, relief and deliverance will arise for the Jews from another place and you and your father's house will perish. And who knows whether you have not attained royalty for such a time as this?"* (Esther 4:13-14 NASB)

Mordecai somehow realizes that this is his last chance; that if he does not find a way to penetrate Esther's defenses, that none of them has a chance of survival. He cannot be sensitive. He cannot mince words. He cannot be politically correct. He cannot even be tactful or polite. He must be clearly, painfully, brutally honest.

He lets her know, in no uncertain terms, that while God can—somehow even in the midst of this impending disaster—save a remnant of Jews through whom He can continue His covenantal purposes; unless she acts immediately, entirely, and courageously, all hope for her, for him, for their people will be lost. He tells Esther that this time, there is no angel coming to save them. There is no plague that is going to ambush their opponents. There is no fire that is going to fall from Heaven and smite their enemies. These things had happened in the past and they may happen in the future, but Mordecai's unequivocal message to his niece is: This time, Esther, it comes down to you.

Lonely, insecure, apprehensive, just-wanting-to-be-loved-and-at-peace you.

You with all your shortcomings and weaknesses and excuses as to why you can't be involved.

You with all your dreams for a calm, easy, comfortable life.

You with the divine favor and blessing that has gotten you this far.

You, Esther, must act; and you must act now. You have been loved, cared for, and blessed for a reason. None of this was about you; it was about what God wanted to do through you. And the time for action is not some far-off day in the future. The time is now. *Right now*. In fact it's now, or never.

~ THE TIME IS NOW. *RIGHT NOW.* ~
IN FACT IT'S NOW, OR NEVER.

As you read about Esther's transformation, we considered that "divine space" between Mordecai's question and Esther's reply. It was in this small yet critical space that she became the Esther we speak of today.

Esther awakened. Esther realized. Esther understood.

Something clicked into gear for Esther, and she recognized that she was part of a much greater plan, a much greater story. Suddenly her personal comfort and security were no longer the determinants in how she would live her life. It was what she could give to this world, not take from it, that would from this point forward, establish her as the heroine of faith she came to be. She knew she had been called to arms, called to action, called to answer the cry of Mordecai. This time *she* would be the angel. *She* would be the miracle. *She* would be the voice that changed darkness into light.

What produced this awakening in her? What was the factor that moved her to put all her chips on the table? I don't know; I don't know that anyone will ever know. But what I do know is that Esther needs to awaken again today.

AWAKENING A CHURCH

Mordecai's dilemma is the same in this day and hour:

- How does one awaken a Church that doesn't know she's asleep?

- How do you get the frog to jump out of the kettle?

Like Esther, we are living in the most urgent of hours, and the Church in the West (especially in the United States) lives in a place of perceived security, protection, and ease. We are distracted and in denial about the fact that an even graver danger than the one threatening the Jews in Susa is threatening us today. However, it is not radical Islam that should serve as the primary source of our concern.

Much of this book has been dedicated to exposing the threat the West faces of a radicalized religious war, that is, by its own admission, on a quest to subject all the world to Shari'ah law. We each have the moral obligation to comprehend and combat this terrifying prospect. But as with anything in life, it is not the external threat that presents the most danger; it is always the enemy within that poses the greatest threat. To focus our grievance on Islam as the culprit of the disturbing state of world affairs would be as foolish as leaving your front door wide open every night, and complaining that your house is repeatedly burglarized. We must get to the root of this issue, not just bat at the branches, if we expect to see the societal transformation we desire.

~ WE MUST GET TO THE ROOT OF THIS ISSUE IF WE EXPECT TO SEE THE SOCIETAL TRANSFORMATION WE DESIRE. ~

Dr. Dmitry Radyshevsky is Director of The Jerusalem Summit, a consortium of world leaders that convenes annually to address the twin dangers facing the West: secular humanism and radical Islam. His remarks from the London 2007 Summit could not make my point any more clearly:

> It may sound ironic that I, a Jew, am calling for a Christian revival in Europe…So excuse my rather immodest and maybe unsolicited advice, but for me the choice for Europe looks very simple. Either it will be a fundamentally Christian Europe or it will be Europe of Islamic Fundamentalists….
>
> …If Europe wishes to save itself, it has to believe in itself as a Christian continent once again; it has to regain absolute confidence that Biblical values are the right values. There is no middle. Europe cannot keep

being hedonistic, atheistic, and neutrally lukewarm in respect to the Bible, including being neutral or even hostile to the task of re-attachment to its Hebrew roots and to Israel. Europeans will be either very hot Christians, burning with faith and Holy Spirit, or they'll be dead cold victims of Islamism.[2]

This modern-day Mordecai is not mincing words either. He cuts to the quick and addresses the complacency running rampant in "Christian society." He says, in effect: If the Church were occupying the place that it should be, there is no chance Islam would be occupying the place that it is. Plato put it much more succinctly, and at a much earlier date: "The price good men pay for indifference to public affairs is to be ruled by evil men."[3]

LIGHT IN THE DARKNESS

From perils without and perils within, it is a dark time for people of faith and goodwill. I believe we are in a night season not unlike the one Esther found herself in. The presence of God is muted, or at best distorted, in many sectors of society and even within the organized Church. The baleful powers conspiring against God's chosen people are even more formidable than they were when Haman etched his plot to annihilate them centuries ago. And in the midst of all of it, what is our response? What is the demonstration that will come forth from the people of God?

Jesus tells His disciples that they are "the light of the world," and that we must not be hidden, but displayed, so that we may give light for all to see (see Matt. 5:14). He goes on to say, *"Let your light so shine before men, that they may see your good works and glorify your Father in heaven"* (Matt. 5:16). Not *His* light; not *Jesus'* light. It is *our* light God wants to shine.

Could it be that without the darkness of bewilderment, distress, and gloom, Esther would not have been compelled to make her inner transformation? Could it be that, for those with eyes of faith, darkness is simply an opportunity to shine?

Indeed, darkness is the backdrop on which the display of our lives is made manifest.

DARKNESS IS THE BACKDROP ON WHICH THE DISPLAY OF OUR LIVES IS MADE MANIFEST.

Esther's Hebrew name (Hadassah) shares the same root as the Hebrew word for *concealment*. Esther was concealed in many ways—seemingly from the eyes of God and, certainly, her true identity as a Jewess was concealed from the eyes of her Persian contemporaries. How fitting then, that the Persian meaning for the name Esther is *star*.

Do you remember learning in elementary school how stars never go away? Contrary to how we tend to think of them, stars don't "come out" at night. They orbit through the same space in our galaxy both night and day. It is only the absence of the vivid light of the brightest star (the sun) that causes their radiance to become visible. This reminds us that seasons of darkness are intrinsically linked with the unmistakable, undeniable, and wholly inconcealable manifestation of light.

I believe God dims the lights at certain moments in which He wants the attention to be on Him. Just when He is ready to move, God wants it quiet—He wants it dark. And since God doesn't move except through His people, that darkness is our entrance cue.

Esther made her appearance, and not a moment too soon. She recognized that she had been positioned in a unique moment, a *kairos* moment, which had to be seized before it passed and was relegated to the realm of what should have, would have, or could have been. She must have known what we know now—that timing is everything; that the opportunities of today, if not acted upon, are the regrets of tomorrow. It must have been this belief that compelled Esther to make the choice she made, to lay her life down in hopes that her people would live to see a better day than she.

She did not commit the common error of thinking that the gathering storm would somehow, eventually blow over. Evil never just goes away. Unless utterly demolished, its powers only multiply and gain strength. Esther must have known this too, as it was the reason she was encountering this calamity to begin with.

Esther and Mordecai were Benjamites, of the same lineage as King Saul. Their ancestor, as a young king, made the mistake of sparing the evil king Agag and not completely wiping out his people the Amalekites (the enemies of the Jews) when God gave him the opportunity to destroy them. (This was due to an ambush the Amalekites had previously perpetrated mercilessly against the ancient Hebrews.)

Because Saul did not fully carry out the orders of God given through Samuel the prophet (see 1 Sam. 15:2-3), the line of the Amalekites continued, eventually leading to the day when Haman, a descendent of King Agag, picked up the centuries-old vendetta against the children of God. Esther was left to finish what should have been done generations before. She determined that this age-old battle would rage no longer; it was going to end with her.

PEACE FOR *ALL* TIME

What one generation doesn't complete, the next is left to finish. To wit, Neville Chamberlain's faulty assurances of "peace for our time" revealed a short-sighted, self-centered perspective that cared for its own generation's comfort rather than the disaster that could quickly follow.

As I reflect on this position, I can't help thinking of Hezekiah's reaction when he learns of the destruction that has been decreed over his house once he departs this life.

219

Essentially Hezekiah's response is, "Well, at least there will be peace in my day" (see 2 Kings 20:19).

Contrast those almost identical blunders to this stance, taken by Winston Churchill.

In June 1940, just after France had fallen to the Axis powers, it was widely feared that Britain would soon follow. Instead of holding onto whatever illusion of security they had left, Prime Minister Churchill, in one of his stirring speeches, rallied the citizens of the United Kingdom to do whatever it took to see that evil advance no farther:

> If we can stand up to him [Hitler], all Europe may be free and the life of the world may move forward into broad, sunlit uplands. But if we fail, then the whole world, including the United States, including all that we have known and cared for, will sink into the abyss of a new Dark Age made more sinister, and perhaps more protracted, by the lights of perverted science. Let us therefore brace ourselves to our duties, and so bear ourselves that if the British Empire and its Commonwealth last for a thousand years, men will still say, "This was their Finest Hour."[4]

Instead of thinking of himself, of personal comfort and personal gain, Churchill thought of the generations to come—"for a thousand years." His desire was that his generation would be the one to sacrificially usher in a new era in British history, preparing the way for the well-being of all the others.

Jewish tradition teaches that there is a Haman who rises up in every generation. Unfortunately this theory is a hard one to refute. But if there is a Haman for every generation, and if the Jewish people are still the thriving presence they are in the earth today, wouldn't it follow that, in every generation, there has also been an Esther as well? This book has been dedicated, in large part, to honoring their memory. But the truest way we can show our admiration of them is by following their lead and making the choices they would make if they were alive today.

~ JEWISH TRADITION TEACHES THAT THERE IS A HAMAN THAT RISES UP IN EVERY GENERATION. UNFORTUNATELY, THIS THEORY IS HARD TO REFUTE. ~

Don't misunderstand me: I'm not calling for another Corrie ten Boom to be raised up. I'm not asking for another Winston Churchill. I'm not wondering when the imperial "Esther" of our day is going to be revealed. Beloved, at this point, it's going to take a lot more than a few isolated individuals who stand for God's Kingdom, His peace, and His righteousness. With the steadily advancing mission of radical secularism, the threat of global domination under the sword of Islam now a not-so-inconceivable prospect, and an ever increasing apathy within the Western Church, it is going to take all of us acting with great courage to see godly change in this hour. Today, we need a *generation* called Esther.

BECOMING AN ESTHER GENERATION

I invite you to lay hold of the five breakthroughs Esther experienced that we may follow in her footsteps.

1. Recognize the Reality

Whose reality are we plugged into? Does our worldview line up with that of the One True God? We must cease ignoring the warning sirens around us, which so many well-meaning people are doing to their own detriment. We must cut ourselves free from our defense mechanisms of distraction and denial and stop telling ourselves *it can't be all that bad*. Whatever we're up against, we're not going to get anywhere unless we come face to face with reality as it truly is.

In pulpits and prayer rooms, in youth groups and women's Bible studies, in college fellowships and pastors' prayer gatherings, we must stop ignoring the elephant in the room. It's not going to do us any good to close our eyes, stop our ears and pull the covers over our heads. We—YOU—must speak out loudly, frequently, truthfully, and decisively.

2. Cry Out

Once we come to terms with reality as it really is, a thousand things are going to vie for our attention. We will be tempted to do it our way, in our own strength. But every earthly victory we win is merely a reflection of a victory already won in the heavenlies. We must humble ourselves and beseech the God of Heaven who says, "My House shall be called a House of Prayer." Instead of thinking potluck dinners, we need to start thinking corporate fasting. Less speculation, more supplication. Less theory, more tears. Whether we're praying to avert certain disaster, or to prepare ourselves for the anti-Christ system that is emerging in the earth, one thing is certain: we must pray and we must not stop.

3. Determine Our Convictions

Being a person of strong moral conviction is not highly valued in our post-modern culture. But throughout time, it has only ever been persons of deep conviction who have accomplished anything.

When faced with her even-though moment, Esther determined her convictions and resolved to do what God was asking of her. We will all, sooner or later, come to a line in the sand. We will all come to our even-though moment—the moment it will actually, genuinely cost us to stand up for what and Who we believe in. Our true convictions lie in what we are willing to do, not merely in what we are willing to profess. So what does your life *say* about you?

4. Have Great Courage

Is courage required of you to live out one typical day in your daily life? If not, you may not be walking out your convictions. In our generation, courage has become more of a myth than a virtue. We need to, as the Body of Christ, rediscover the lost art of courage, which rightly belongs to the household of God.

We must draw from the legacy of biblical and contemporary heroes for inspiration and endeavor to stand for what is right with our lives, and if needful, our deaths. I have small children, and daily question the level of security in the world they are growing up in. Instead of allowing this to move me to the sidelines, however, I purpose, every day, to live in such a way that the world I am leaving them is the one it should be.

5. Receive Divine Strategy

God really does have a plan, and He is all too eager to share it with us. *"If any of you lacks wisdom, let him ask of God, who gives to all liberally and without reproach, and it will be given to him"* (James 1:5). We are drowning in good ideas; but what we need are *God* ideas. Whoever would have thought that throwing a small dinner party would reverse a death decree written for an entire nation? But we serve a God who delights to partner with His creation and use the natural elements in our hands to accomplish supernatural feats.

The greatest warfare strategy of all is to focus not on engaging your enemy, but entertaining your King. If we will honor the Lord, wait on Him in prayer, and seek His wisdom, He really will give us the strategies needed to advance His Kingdom.

THE TURNING

I encourage you to read for yourself the Book of Esther and allow the Holy Spirit's Mordecai cry to enter your heart in a deeper way. The end of the book is really the best, and it is often what is most easily skipped over. The victory the Jews in Susa experienced is legendary and is still celebrated by the Jewish people today.

The Feast of Purim is a joyous celebration for the Jews, which commemorates the day marked out for their destruction, when they instead wreaked havoc on their enemies and were established by God in peace and triumph. During traditional Purim observances to this day, each time the name of Haman is mentioned in the proceedings, the crowd shouts, "Venahafoch hu!" which means, "The tables were turned!" Or, "The opposite happened!" This lively custom comes from Esther 9:1b, which says, "On the day that the enemies of the Jews had hoped to overpower them, *the opposite occurred*, in that the Jews themselves overpowered those who hated them."

The opposite happened. The tables turned. Haman hung on the gallows he built for Mordecai. Instead of annihilation, the Jews advanced. Instead of decreasing in number, they gained followers. If there was ever a lesson from history that needed a modern-day application, it's this one. We need to see a *turning of the tide* in the nations of the earth. We need to become the force we were created to be. We must become an Esther Generation. We must become the answer to our own prayers.

> IF THERE WAS EVER A LESSON FROM
> ~ HISTORY THAT NEEDED A MODERN- ~
> DAY APPLICATION, IT'S THIS ONE.

Haman was one individual who almost destroyed a nation. Esther was one individual who saved a nation. And you are one individual whose story is not yet finished. Will you hear the cry of Mordecai?

Maybe your even-though moment won't make CNN, but I can assure you, your Maker and Redeemer is tuned into your every move and is avidly watching to see you become all He has destined you to be.

I am not saying it will be easy. I am not even guaranteeing our actions will bring about our desired result. Esther didn't know how things would turn out, and neither do I. All I know is that, like Esther, we have been blessed unto purpose.

An orphan girl from Susa answered the cry.

Will we?

ENDNOTES

1. http://freedomkeys.com/quotations.htm.

2. http://www.jerusalemsummit.org/eng/js_london_radyshevsky.php; accessed 9/2/08.

3. http://www.quoteland.com/topic.asp?CATEGORY_ID=331; accessed 9/2/08.

4. http://www.winstonchurchill.org/i4a/pages/index.cfm?pageid=388#Finest; accessed 9/2/08.

A CALL TO ACTION

If this book has done its job, then you will be stirred to action. You will be moved to do something different, something new; something of action will come from the words you have read.

Thankfully, there are a growing number of individuals around the world who are hearing the cry of Mordecai and are being roused to action. People from every walk of life, every background; people just like you, who in their own way, are making a difference every day in the world around them.

At Eagles' Wings, we desire to connect and partner with you during these momentous times in history. Please browse our Website at www.eagleswings.to and see some of the many ways you can be involved to make a difference in Israel and the nations. Also, please be sure to sign up for our e-mail updates and to send us your contact information so that we can be in touch with you regarding corporate action. The following are a few of the many "action steps" you can take to respond to Mordecai's cry. God is doing so many works through so many people in this critical hour; here are some of them:

DAY OF PRAYER FOR THE PEACE OF JERUSALEM (DPPJ)

Now that you have heard the cry of Mordecai, help others hear it too! Become a DPPJ Coordinator for your local church, city, or region, encouraging believers in your sphere of influence to join millions of others on the first Sunday of every October, to pray for the peace of Jerusalem and for all of her people. Decide now to become a voice for Jerusalem and Israel in your region, by sharing with others about this global grassroots movement and of the importance of standing with Israel today. You can find more information about this strategic prayer initiative, plus download free DPPJ resources, by visiting www.daytopray.com.

CHRISTIANS UNITED FOR ISRAEL

Be part of a united voice for Israel and Jewish people worldwide. Join your efforts with those of Christians United for Israel (CUFI), a grassroots initiative that has been sweeping across America under the direction of Pastor John Hagee and thousands of Jewish and Christian leaders. As a member of CUFI, you will not only have the opportunity to stay informed on current news and initiatives with respect to Israel and the West, but you will also have the opportunity to lobby with others in Washington, DC, for your congressmen to pass legislation that stands unequivocally with Israel. Visit www.cufi.org.

NIGHTS TO HONOR ISRAEL

Participate in Nights to Honor Israel, evening events that take place every year across the United States to demonstrate

Christians' support of and love for Israel. To find a Night to Honor Israel coming soon to your area, please visit www.cufi.org.

ISRAEL EXPERIENCE COLLEGE SCHOLARSHIP

If you are (or know of) a college or university student who is serious about getting trained and equipped on current issues in the Middle East and how they affect your future and your world, I urge you to prayerfully consider the Israel Experience College Scholarship Program (IE). This unique opportunity provides a three-week intensive experience in the land of Israel that gives the best and brightest Christian students an educated heart for Israel and her people. Meeting face to face with governmental, religious, and educational leaders from the diverse people groups in that land, IE students are equipped with both experience and knowledge to be a voice for Israel on their college campuses and in their future careers.

If you are not a student yourself, you can still be involved in this amazing program by helping sponsor a student. Visit our Website at www.daytopray.com or call our office at 1-800-51-WINGS.

WATCHMEN ON THE WALL

Curriculum. Become an informed intercessor and an articulate voice for Israel and the Jewish people by participating in the Watchmen on the Wall Training Program. A broad-based but structured curriculum written by knowledgeable Christian leaders, with a variety of relevant material and assignments. Resources include a Watchmen Manual which could be called an "Israel 101 Primer," plus three volumes of audio training CDs with PowerPoint presentation to supplement and enhance the material in the manual. All Watchmen training resources are available online at www.daytopray.com under Bookstore.

Trip. Eagles' Wings Watchmen on the Wall Pilgrimages to Israel are unique trips to the Holy Land. You will not only see what God did there thousands of years ago; you will be impacted and challenged by what God is doing there today. If you also complete the curriculum portion of the Watchmen on the Wall program prior to making the pilgrimage, you can be personally commissioned by the city of Jerusalem and the state of Israel as an official Watchman on the Wall—one released by governmental and religious authorities in the Holy Land to be an effective intercessor and a competent spokesman for Israel and her people. For more information, visit www.daytopray.com and click on Watchmen on the Wall.

Seminar. Host a Watchmen on the Wall seminar in your local church, and awaken others to the realities facing our generation. These educational seminars are an excellent resource, taught by outstanding teachers. Contact our offices at office@eagleswings.to for information on how your church or regional network can host a Watchmen on the Wall seminar in your area, or to find out where there is a Watchmen seminar in your area to attend.

Other resources. Keepers of the Flame by Robert Stearns, published by Kairos Publishing 2003. *Watchmen on the Wall Manual* (2006) by Kairos Publishing.

The God who calls you by name is also the God of all creativity; He can call you to a totally different action that is not listed above, but is uniquely fitting to your gifts, your experience, and your sphere of influence. Allow the Holy Spirit cry of Mordecai to enter your spirit, and become the Esther you are called to be.

"Yet who knows whether you have come to the Kingdom for such a time as this?"

Shalom,
Robert Stearns

For everyone to whom much is given,
from him much will be required;
and to whom much has been committed,
of him they will ask the more

(Luke 12:48b).

EAGLES' WINGS

Eagles' Wings is an international relational network of believers, churches, and ministries committed to the lifestyle of biblical spirituality through a lifestyle of worship and prayer, the unity of the Body of Christ, and the restoration of Israel.

Eagles' Wings is comprised of a full-time staff of 60, under the leadership of an advisory board with Robert Stearns serving as Executive Director. Eagles' Wings has ministered in over 30 nations, and maintains active, ongoing ministry in Honduras and Israel.

PO Box 450
Clarence, NY 14031

Tel: 716-759-1058
Fax: 716-759-0731

Visit our Websites:
www.eagleswings.to
www.daytopray.com
www.kairos.org

Additional copies of this book and other
book titles from DESTINY IMAGE are
available at your local bookstore.

Call toll-free: 1-800-722-6774.

Send a request for a catalog to:

Destiny Image® Publishers, Inc.

P.O. Box 310
Shippensburg, PA 17257-0310

*"Speaking to the Purposes of God for this
Generation and for the Generations to Come."*

**For a complete list of our titles,
visit us at www.destinyimage.com.**